THE TENTH WONDER OF THE WORLD

THE TENTH WONDER OF THE

WORLD

JERRY L. RHOADS

ISBN:	Softcover	978-1-5245-2328-2
	eBook	978-1-5245-2327-5

Print information available on the last page.

Rev. date: 09/06/2016

To order additional copies of this book, contact:
Xlibris
1-888-795-4274
www.Xlibris.com
Orders@Xlibris.com
738363

CONTENTS

PREFACE.....xvii
INTRODUCTION.....xxi
DAY DREAM.....1

AUTHOR'S SEVEN WONDERS OF THE WORLD.....3

THESE ARE THE SEVEN WONDERS OF THE PHYSICAL WORLD VIEWED FROM OUTER SPACE.....4
THESE ARE THE SEVEN WONDERS OF THE INVISIBLE WORLD TO VIEW INNER SPACE.....5
WONDERS OF THE WORLD.....6
THE TENTH WONDER OF THE WORLD.....9
BELIEVE THE WONDERS.....11
THE LAND.....13
DARK HORSE (DH) WHITE HOUSE.....16
THE WHITE HOUSE.....19
THE COMMON CENTS OF IT ALL.....22
THAT SPECIAL BREED.....25
MY YELLOW CONVERTIBLE.....27
WARREN COUNTY FAIR.....29

THE EDGE OF THE FOREST.....31

THE EDGE OF THE FOREST.....32
GIVE HER A CHANCE.....36
WELL HEALED.....38
POTLATCH.....40
FREEDOM.....43
FUTURE INHERITED.....45
SUPER BOWL MONDAY.....47

BON APPETITE 50
STATUS 52
HITTING THE RAILS 54
A HISTORY ON THE RUN 55
STILL WATERS 56
THIS IS NOT GOODBYE 57

X WHERE GOOD CROSSES BAD 59

X MARKS THE SPOT
WHERE GOOD crosses BAD 61
MY BEST FRIEND 63
RUNNING FROM LIFE 64
HOME STEAD 66
FAMILY BY ANOTHER NAME 68
SEARCHING 71
DEEPER THOUGHT 73
HOURGLASS 75
DOUBLE TROUBLE
SEEING DOUBLE 79
A WORTHY THORN 81
SCALES 83
SLEEPING ALONE 85
NEVER LOOK BACK 87
LIFE IN A TENT 89
MY LOVE WALKED ON 91
RECEIVING CAN YOU GIVE 93
MEET THE CHALLENGE 95
I THEE WED 97

THE CIRCUS 101

THE CIRCUS 103
LISTEN OR LEARN 105
SANDBOX 107
PUFF AND I'M GONE 110
MELTING RAIN 112
SIESTA MOTEL 113
BEDROOM EYES 115

ON STANDBY 117
THE TIME HAS COME 119
DOESN'T MATTER NONE 121
NO ORDINARY MEN 123
SOMEDAY MORNING 126
LOVINGTOWN 128
A DAY IN THE LIFE 130
WHO LIES HERE 132
THEY MISTOOK 134

I CAN FLY 137

I CAN FLY 139
THE MENTALITY OF LOVE 141
FRECKLES 143
NO ONE KNOWS 145
EATING WITH THE CROWS 147
THE GOOD EARTH 149
ONE BRICK AT A TIME 151
I WENT ON DOWN TO THE CITY 153
FOR IN THINE WILL 155
RUMORS AREN'T TRUTH 157
BUMBLE BEE 159
BIRTH OF REALITY 161
DRY RAIN 163
THE WIZZARD OF WORDS 165
NICKNAMED 167
THE SHIELD 170
NEVER CAN WAIT 172
LIFE BALL 174
SCHOOL DAYS 176

ELVIS IS DEAD 177

ELVIS IS DEAD 179
SIDER WEB 181
THE OLD BRICK ROAD 183
ACE OF EIGHTS 185
THE POET 186

LONELY TRAVELING MAN 187
SHADOWS 189
INKY AND PEPPY 191
GET OFF MY DOCK 193
HIM AND HER 195
DEATH OF CAMELOT 197
PAPER ROUTE 200
THE ELEVENTH COMMANDMENT NO MORTAL SHALL BEG 202
OIL ON WATER 204
SPIDERS AND BEES 206
IN A SECOND 208
TO FASHION 210

MY LIFE KITE 213

MY LIFE KITE 215
DISTANCE 217
THE SON OF A FATHER 219
MUTUAL 221
HIGH SCHOOL REUNION 223
IDLE TALK 225
CATCH ME IF YOU CAN 227
AS TIME RAN COLD 229
LIFESTYLES 231
WHO SAID LOVE IS FAIR 233
PAST TENSE 235
LUFKIN 2526 237
REHIREMENT 239
POET or WRITER 241
ALONE TOGETHER 243
COWARD 245
BOTTOMS UP 247
DIGNITY 249

GOLD DIGGER 251

GOLD DIGGER 253
DRIVEN 255
SONGWRITER BLUES 256

HALF OF THEM 258
LIFE SUSTAINING 260
SING YOUR OWN SONG 262
EMOTIONS 264
SAYINGS 266
THE POET IN ME 268
THE MAKER AND THE UNDERTAKER IN US ALL 270
PUMPING GAS 272
BUILD HOPE 273
A HEART OF GOLD 274
HABITS TOO HIGH OR LOW 276
HURRY 278
THE SAME DIFFERENCE 280
LOOK ALIKE 282
LOVE HAS NO LIMIT 284
INFINITY 286

FAIREST OF THEM ALL 289

FAIREST OF THEM ALL 291
THE IVORY TOWER 294
ARE YOU LISTENING 296
TOMORROW A MAN 298
EMOTIONS 301
AS TIME PASSES 303
WORST HAIRCUT 305
FRIENDS OF A FEATHER 307
COTTON CANDY HEAVEN 310
IF THE CLOCK DOESN'T TICK 312
LOVER'S HIGH 313
I'D BE NOTHING 315
WHAT LITTLE GLORY 316

THE BIRTHING OF THE NATION 319

THE BIRTHING OF THE NATION 321
IN MY WILDEST DREAMS 323
THE TIME HAD COME 325
INFLATION AND STAGNATION 327

Deflation 329
HIGH ON LIFE 330
REASON OR RESULT 332
IN MY BLOOD 334
DREAMS BECOME REALITY 336
TO SERVE 338
THE LOVE I HAVE 340
WE ALL COME FROM THE SAME SEED 342
CIERZO (THE WIND) 344

INNER PERSUASION 347

INNER PERSUASION 349
EVOLUTION 351
THE MOMENT OF LOVE 353
TALK IS CHEAP 355
SEASONS WITH YOU 357
THE LOOK OF LOVE 359
CHICKEN LITTLE'S THREAT 361
I THOUGHT I KNEW YOU 363
LOVE'S INCISIONS 365
MY HEART TELLS NO LIES 366

LIFE'S CLIMB 369

LIFE'S CLIMB 371
DESTINY 373
BORN TO BE EQUAL 375
PERFECT LOVE 379
HALFTIME 381
CAR SICK 383
I BELIEVE 386
GIFTS 387
BOTTOM OF THE DECK 388

THE CREST 391

THE CREST 392
THE WHITES OF THEIR EYES 394

DUMPING GROUNDS....396
REASON TO CONFESS....398
MICE AND MEN....400
THE PILGRIM....401
EYE TO EYE....403
TURN HOMEWARD....404
LIFE OF A PUPPET....405
ODE OF KELLI JO....407
LONNIE AND DONNIE....409
MORALITY....413
AN EXPRESSION....414
THE SAME SKY....415

HOME FOR THE HOLIDAYS....417

HOME FOR THE HOLIDAYS....419
CHRISTMAS....420
CELEBRATING THE NEW YEAR....422
EASTER....424
MEMORIAL DAY....427
THE FOURTH OF JULY
INDEPENDENCE DAY....428
LABOR DAY
HARVEST THE SOUL....429
THANKSGIVING....431
STOP FIGHTING LOVE....433
MOTHERS AND DAUGHTERS....435
SIGNS....437
THE GOSPEL SINGER....439
I WALKED THE BEACH....442
ATOM and EVE....444
THE RHOADS THEOREM....445
OLD FASHIONED BOY....447
GIVE ME MY RIGHTS....449
MRS. RAPP'S RABBIT TRAP....451
AN EXTRA MILE....453

THE SEA TAKETH 455

THE SEA TAKETH 457
I SAW GOD 459
INTESTINAL AGEITUDE 461
WON'T BUY MY LOVE 463
LIVING BY SUBJECTIVES 465
THE FRIEND SHIP 467
A SMILE 468
MY SON 469
WHO CARES 470
EVERY MAN AND WOMAN 472
JOEY IS 474
THE MIND OF MAN 476
A UNIQUE OPPORTUNITY 478
IT'S GONE 480
THE CAGE 482
RIDING IN BACK 484

I SAW YOU STANDING THERE 487

I SAW YOU STANDING THERE 489
WITHOUT MEANING 492
WATER TO THE TREE 494
SOME PEOPLE 495
TELL ME WHY 497
A REGAL EAGLE 498
BEING LOST 500
HOLD MY HAND 502
IT HURTS ME 504
TALK IS CHEAP 505
IT'S BY DESIGN 506
THE CONCEPTION 507
BETTER THAN ME 508
EYE OF THE HURRICANE 509
THE CHILDREN SAID NO 511
THE SPRINGTIME OF OUR LIVES 513
SANDMAN 515

STONED SOBER **517**

STONED SOBER 519
HOLD ME TILL I CRY 521
HAPPINESS IS 522
WHAT WOULD YOU DO 524
THE TEN COMMANMENTS OF LOVE 526
ETERNITY 527
NUMBER ONE 528
FOR THE PERSISTENT 530
FOR THE INSISTENT 531
PEOPLE ARE PEOPLE 532
DIFFERENT 534
THE MIND GARDENER 536
A SET BACK 537
END OF BEGINNINGS 539
REPLAY ME 540
PURITY 542
ALIBIS 544

MY SHADOW **547**

MY SHADOW 549
THE ME SOCIETY 552
DESTINY 554
MOTHER NATURE 555
WITNESS 556
DESOLATE OR VIBRANT 558
THE PAUPER'S LEDGER 560
TAINTED GLASS 562
EMPTY ARMS 564
STAIN ON MY PILLOW 566
NOT TOO OLD TO LOVE 568
GIVE TO GET 569
NOVENNA 571

DON'T WALK ON MY GRAVE **575**

DON'T WALK ON MY GRAVE 577
SAVE ME 579
AGING FACES 580
SHEBA 582
MAN GRAVE 584

CRYSTAL BALL **585**

CRYSTAL BALL 587
LIFE AS AN ICICLE 589
LISTEN TO THE WORLD TURN 590
FALLING STAR 592
CROOKED FOOTPRINTS 594
SMILE ME A RAINBOW 596
COMPETITORS 597

THE AUTUMN OF OUR LIVES **601**

THE AUTUMN OF OUR LIVES 603
BAD BOSS BLUES 604
HEAVEN ON EARTH 606
A LIBRA 607
EVERGREEN 609
THE DAY YOU TOLD ME GOODBYE 610
THE EMBARRASSED RIVER 612
PARENTS KNOW 614
COMING DOWN 617
HOPE LIGHTS MY FIRE 619

FOOL'S GOLD **621**

FOOL'S GOLD 623
LIVE AS A TREE 625
MY LOVELY 627
CARTWHEELS 629
THAT'S ROMANCE 631
ON THE WINGS OF THE DOVE 633
PLAY ME 636

WHAT WOULD IT BE....638
PAINT ME A RAINBOW....640
GRADUATION OF SMOKE....643

BROKEN WINDMILLS....645

BROKEN WINDMILLS....647
180 YESTERDAYS....649

FATHER NOAH....651

FATHER NOAH....653
ECLIPSE....656
THE END IS THE BEGINNING....658

PREFACE

My first published poetry book The Eighth Wonder of the World was motivated by the wonder of the mind that we all possess. In the NINTH WONDER OF THE WORLD *it was about poetry combined with photography is the wonderful things we can do with the undiscovered planet called the mind and the magic of the heart.*

In the previous book I used the word God 362 times and faith 53 times though I tend to be an agnostic skeptic. However, in THE NINTH WONDER OF THE WORLD *a sequel to* THE EIGHTH WONDER OF THE WORLD *I write that each man and woman must discover their own* WORLD *and faith. Their life is about the results not the reason for living strong with our physical bodies revolving around a hot sun and wonder-ing under a cold moon how we got here and where it's taking us. What more can a poet asked for to write about if not to wonder how my own world is connected to the* TENTH WONDER OF THE WORLD.

Life is both warm and cold sometimes hot sometimes bold. It depends on each of us and our circumstances that either enhances or detracts from our dreams. But always we make our own reality by our choices and rejoice our gladness or our sadness. Of the 8 billion people on this planet not a one is exactly a replica of another… we have genetically puzzled the PhD's and scientists into submission and are not solving how a bug can have a brain and sex drive but no other individual powers except survival weapons… and half of us reject evolution as a part of the answer… and the rest pray to a spirit that formed us and is in charge of directing our future. Both are assumptive at best. In this book answers are proposed to questions never asked… this is graffiti of the Universal miracle of the planet called the mind that connects us all to that elusive answer to who is God… the brain and heart are physical, the mind and soul are metaphysical connecting us to the WONDERS OF OUR UNIVERSE *called God.*

As In THE EIGTHTH AND NINTH WONDERS OF THE WORLD *each title is a short story with a topical heading, a poetic body and a profound ending that hopefully meets the readers' comprehension and understanding and appreciation. If not, then stimulate thoughts of life and the pursuit of happiness.*

Shari Rhoads, my wife and editor was not that interested in poetry as a good read until she helped me go through every poem and word it to make sense without being vulgar or verbose. She now loves the end product and its meaning to her. Many of the topics are words that come to mind about life and it tribulations that were spoken into a tape recorder thirty some years ago while driving a million miles throughout Illinois servicing my company's accounts.

Typed by my secretary Jane from the player onto beige typing sheets with an old style typewriter in the 12 three ring binders I kept them in for later use that meant no digital copies for the publisher… from time to time I would point them out to our children and grandchildren but with little if no interest.

So here we are into the thirteen binders as the trigger for a published poem or prose or song or drama. With this book I am about half way through the mass of thoughts, truisms, motivating phrases, love, hopes, fears, doubts, spirits, Gods, good government, bad government, criminal minds, happiness, health, prosperity and more. If nothing else I'm prolific. By using the spoken word as the starting point I believe this achieves a more interesting poem because it is as the reader and I speak… with contractions, hem's and ha's, laughs and frets, colloquialisms and sayings, idealism and super stardom, and about our personal fears, dreams and love making.

I had forgotten the joy of writing. Business reports, accounting books, documents for clients, politics, policies and procedures have dominated my mind and output. Now with this median creativity creeps back into my daily routine… picking out a few at a time to input and review as output of a story not a boring business exercise.

My children have become good writers and are appreciating the poetry books more because it is a reflection of their father's thoughts, emotions, desires, goals, disappointments, and dedication to my wife, children, grandchildren and now a great grandson.

Most Men consider poetry and prose a chick thing until they need to convey their feelings in an emotional meaningful way… or a greeting card for birthdays, holidays and anniversaries that use poetry and prose as its entire mode of expression. Even the calendars, hit songs, political speeches, weddings, funerals use poetry as its genesis. So grin and bear it and you may like it.

My daughter Kimber Leigh got her copy and said she intended to give it a look and two hours later she had to put it down and go to bed and go to work. My son Kip said he finally got to read the real me rather than a business version of me. I must admit that females are much more interested in the content and picking up that coffee table ornament... it has to catch a man when catch can. Even that rhymes. If this edition gets to your coffee table then I have succeeded if not use it as a filler on your computer table as a work of digital art. Thanks for taking the time to give it a chance.

INTRODUCTION

What inspired you to write this third poetry book? I have been writing poetry for sixty years. I have had some published in poetry contests but never published collections of my own. My inspiration came from my mother who was a poet, my sister is a playwright, my son is a song writer and musician, my daughters are artists and write poems so I had to step up with something creative since my previous books were all business subjects.

Poetry is so personal it is hard to convince readers to take the time to feel the words not just read them. The Eighth Wonder of the World, my first poetry book, presents something we all possess and don't realize its value. So for this second book to resonate with the buyer/reader a love of poetry will initially be the reason it sells… after that it will be the value to each reader as they capitalize on the Eighth Wonder they possess.

What is the overall theme (central topic, subject or concept) of your book? The Eighth Wonder is the first poem and the theme for my first poetry book. I reveal in that poem what the eighth wonder is and its value to each person on earth. I don't want it revealed until they read that first poem and hopefully will use that Eighth Wonder to find the other wonders of the world… then read the rest of THE NINTH AND TENTH WONDERS OF THE WORLD *exercising their* EIGHTH WONDER *asset.*

Where does this book take place? It resides inside every person on earth.

Who are the main characters and why are they important to the story? The characters are every person on earth pursuing the wonders of the world.

Why do you think that this book will appeal to readers? It delves into most every ology (a subject of study)…. Theology, biology, geography, psychology, astrology, anthropology, ology, ideology, chronology, physiology, meteorology, sociology, etc. That is the power of the Eighth Wonder each of us possess for delving into the over 1 million words in the English language. I the author and the book are the enabler for this study of humanity.

How is your book relevant in today's society? Thought is the most powerful weapon we each have for making a difference in the world. The Eighth Wonder will stimulate that thought process whether it is accepting or rejecting the thoughts presented. THE TENTH WONDER OF THE WORLD *capitalizes on the breadth of the topics and the twists and turns of the Eighth and Ninth Wonders.*

Is there any subject currently trending in the news that relates to your books? Politics, war, peace, leadership, health of the nation… over 2,500 subjects intended to stimulate thinking, understanding and knowledge.

What makes your books different from other books like it? I googled the title and the Eighth Wonder of the World and it gives me a travel guide not a poetry book. So it's unique in its totally title and content. Also it makes the reader exercise their brain in a positive way. Each poem is a story about that subject and is personalized by letting the reader make their own interpretation of that subject.

What do you want readers to take away from your writing? Poems are short stories with a subject, a plot where the end of every poem there is a concluding sentence that sums up the meaning to the author who wants the reader to go WOW *I see… said the blind man as he picked up his hammer and saw. Some tongue in cheek and others meant to be profound to the reader, if at all possible.*

How did you learn about the topic? (i.e. personal experience, education, etc.) Since I have personally experienced the Wonders of the World it is easy for me to write from and about them. I am an aspiring author, not a schooled technician, so most of the poems are from the heart not the head. As I state above and in the introduction to the book all of the poems started with a tape recording of the basic theme and put down on paper by my secretary then put into a three ring binder and thirty some years later entered into my computer to produce the final product. My first two WONDER *books and this collection of poems are only a portion of a total of about 2,500 dictated and the basis for the published books. Not all of them merit publishing so I have to be selective and choosy as I am working on the fourth book with a working title of... make a guess... "Eleventh Wonder of the World".*

Is there a particular passage from this book you'd like us to utilize? If so, please provide me a release form for approval. The first poem in my poetry books set the ball in motion for pursuing the ology's and subjects... while the table of contents directs the reader to subjects of their choosing and each poem is a story for them to enjoy and analyze. Interwoven throughout the 700+ pages are sectional tabs and images for the reader to use to pause for a diversion or picture of my thoughts. So its unique in its tally title and content

What other books have I written?

- a. *The Eighth Wonder of the World (first poetry book)*
- b. *The Ninth Wonder of the World (second poetry book)*
- c. *The Tenth Wonder of the world (third poetry book)*
- d. *The Eleventh Wonder of the world (next poetry book)*
- e. *The Twelfth Wonder of the World (the last sequel to the Wonders of the World)*
- f. *The Boomers Are Coming (a self-heath book)*
- g. *Never Too Old to Live (a self-heath book)*
- h. *America in the Red Zone (a self-heath book)*
- i. *Restore Elder Pride (a self-heath book)*
- j. *Remedy Eldercide (a self-heath book)*
- k. *The Monopsony Game (a economic analysis)*
- l. *Failing Government Taketh Away (a political analysis)*
- m. *American Enterprise Manifesto (a government analysis)*
- n. *Basic Accounting and Budgeting for Long Term Care Facilities*
- o. *Americania 1984 2084 2184 (a novel remembering George Orwell)*
- p. *Mancology (the science of managing human value)*
- q. *Cost Accounting for Long term care facilities*

Do you have an existing website? Yes. web address www.americanenterpriseparty.com

DAY DREAM

By Velma Lou Rhoads (my mother who was a poet)

I built my castle in the sand
A haven just for me
With each room I carefully planned
My sand castle by the sea

Glittering sand castle in the sun
Just a haven built by me
To hold my dreams one by one
My sand castle by the sea

But when I returned one day
To the haven just for me
The winds and tide had swept away
My sand castle by the sea

There was only the barren beach
No haven there for me
The idle dreams were out of reach
My sand castle lay in the sea

AUTHOR'S SEVEN WONDERS OF THE WORLD

THESE ARE THE SEVEN WONDERS OF THE PHYSICAL WORLD VIEWED FROM OUTER SPACE

The Great Wall of China
Steps across the highlands

The Taj Mahal of India
Mausoleum of Mumtaz Mahal

Christ the Redeemer of Brazil
Forgiveness of the savior

The Coliseum of Rome
Gladiators fight for the right to live

Stonehenge of United Kingdom
Outer space travelers or inner space wonders

The Citadel of Haiti
Holy art though

The Great Pyramid of Giza
Wonders of engineering and strength

THESE ARE THE SEVEN WONDERS OF THE INVISIBLE WORLD TO VIEW INNER SPACE

Computers
Makes the invisible visible

Cell phones
Makes the decibels hearable

Television
Makes the unseen seen

Electric Robot Autos
Burns neutrons not gas

Lasers
For seeing through time

Satellites
GPS and all its wonders

Drones
The robots of the air ways

WONDERS OF THE WORLD

Undiscovered thoughts
Unused words that rhyme
Unspent moments in time
What a crime
The tenth planet is left spinning
In the brine

What is this thing of you speak
Is it about today
Or is it next week
Prophet tell me, its answers I seek
What is this wonder
You ponder

"Well it's a planet alright
Carried with you day and night
Many have found it
And are using it right
To be perceptive
And somewhat bright"

Like the tenth planet
This psychic wonder
Is owned by every man and woman
They've had it since birth
So they could walk and wander
Left to their willingness and worth
At hand to accept or squander

A nearby diamond
At ready commands
Unspoken words and schemes
Misused ideas and plans
Broken dreams, ranting pleas
And if by chance
Lost to its mental disease
It's a wonder, a haven

Numbering eight billion
Beyond the reaches of heaven
Determining our fate
To use before it's too late
Spinning our own DNA web
As the sign, of that mental state
Linking us to the spiritual ebb
Of our immortal fate

For all of mankind
To find their Eighth Wonder
Called the mind

For all of mankind
To find their Ninth Wonder
Called the Soul

Connecting us all to the sublime
A metaphysical Solar system divine

The brain and the heart are physical,
The mind and the soul are metaphysical connecting
All of us to the Tenth Wonder of our Universe called the heart

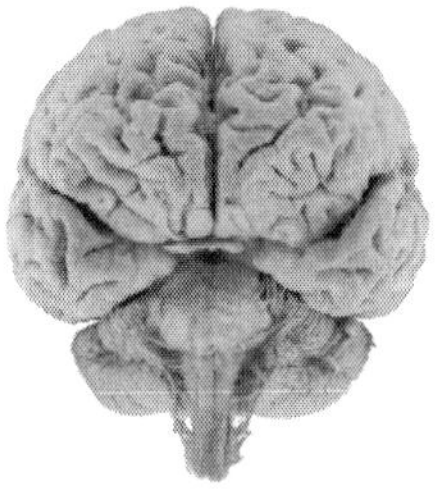

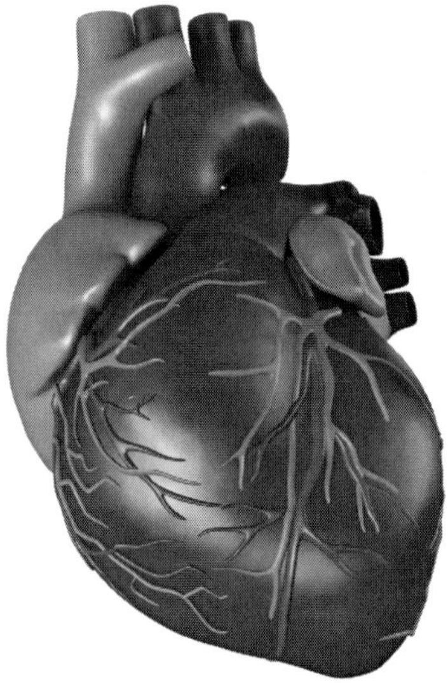

THE TENTH WONDER OF THE WORLD

Contemplate procrastinate prophet gate
The wonders of the world
8 billion inhabitants of the world
And none alike

100 trillion ants in the world
Weighing in as much as humans
With a heart dorsal aorta
Ants have heart too

17 quadrillion flies in the world
Weighing in as much as humans
With a brain Cerebral Ganglia
Flies have a brain too

600,000 monkeys in the world
Weighing in as much as
10 million heads of a pen
Monkeys have soul too

500,000 apes in the world
Weighing in at 1.2% difference
Genome than humans
Apes have a mind too

You my friend have all four
Functioning at once forever
In a World Solar System
Universal Galaxy and Cosmos

All in your own space
90 Atoms in your cells
37.2 trillion cells in your body
100 MILLION neurons in your brain

Revolving around in your own self-contained spiritual world

The human heart is the nucleus... this is truly
the Tenth Wonder of the World

For all of mankind
To find their Eighth Wonder
Called the mind

For all of mankind
To find their Ninth Wonder
Called the Soul

For all of mankind
To find their Tenth Wonder
Called the heart

Connecting us all to the sublime
A metaphysical Solar system divine

The brain and the heart are physical,
The mind and the soul are metaphysical connecting
All of us to the Tenth Wonder of our
personal Universe called the heart

BELIEVE THE WONDERS

The Wonders of Earth:
The sky clouds sun birds land soil earth mountains
streams snow plains meadows flowers sea salt sails

The Wonders of Life:
Sight feeling smelling tasting touching loving DNA cells birth death

The Wonders of Space:
Comets sun spots planets sun moon black
hole atoms E=MC2 continuums

Tis all wrapped up in one round ball
Hung upon a trespass of the universe
This round ball called Earth so unique
So unique it boggles the mortal mind if answers you seek
That black cavern we know as the infinite space
Marked by stars set in place
Unique maybe it's a freak of Mother Nature
As God allows seasons to speak

Something had to happen to place us here
Far Far Far away not so near
The miracles of life oh so dear
Inhabitants of this sphere
Plants insects reptiles mammals birds and human peer

Sundown and sunup marks the celebration
At the wonder of our life… it's a sensation
The very distance of this will
Narrow the human mind to something small
But maybe just maybe the truth
Of this tiny ball called Earth
Is that it's just the core of much more
Likely given birth layers upon layers
Like a diamond onion or tree's girth

If this be true the value of life should occur to you
We then become the center of something much bigger
Not just the bough or the out rigger
Tis the very wonder of life that
Some cosmic atom colliding created
Not to be apart or ever separated

Be it a big bang or a big God
This round ball we plod
Is all we've got
Unless we expand the plot
With the pull of gravity
The White Hole the womb
Opens the door
To much more
The Black Hole the tomb
Closes the door
To evermore

Then we are dealing with the
Expanse of infinity
Merely the trip of the human
Spirit after death to eternity

Believe what you will
Or disbelieve
The Wonders of it all
Makes us all believers

In the unbelievable

THE LAND

The land upon which we walk
The land upon which our boot heels tread
The land upon which our hands guide the stalk
The land upon which we lay our dead

This land is ours while we're here
This land will give as much as it can take
This is why we must hold it oh so dear
Leaving it in place for our children's sake

The land is so beautiful in the spring
Holding to its breast the voice of nature
Uplifting with life to bring
For without it there would be no creature

We cultivate its fertility
We seem to ignore its scarcity
We find hope in its stability
And when it's over we inherit its sanctity

In the summer we watch the crops
Bloom into the harvests
Hoping that the cycle never stops
Providing food to feed our nests

Its green and black skin is only the surface
God is there no doubt
Beneath is our spirit and our purpose
Spreading life all about

In the fall as the leaves settle to the land
Getting ready to go to sleep
Why don't mortals understand
Why nature's children need peace to keep

Times have told us to feed the land
Don't forsake it just for today
Replenish thus our contraband
Lest the very soul of man will decay

As the winter curtain drops its veil
Over the eyes of those that hibernate
The cycle slows to almost stale
Putting us humans in a blissful state

The land must stand and never fall
The land is the very roots of everything
The land is the soul of mother father of all
The land has so much more to which we cling

So dig the dirt and drop the seed
Pick its fruit
And curse its weed
But please don't forego the need

To sing out to nature's creed
"Your land is my land
Yours to till at my will
If you use it
God be damned if you
Abuse it"

With this statement of inconvenient truth
Supported by all even the youth
That our Good Earth
Must sustain its natural worth

Through our committed conservation
Reading the signs of deterioration
Knowing salvation isn't deprivation
But needs an alliance of each nation

To serve Mother Nature's value
As all individuals conserve
Then preserve her
For our very survival's nerve

Each to his own way
The land holds all on Judgement Day

DARK HORSE (DH)
WHITE HOUSE

Ride a dark horse
Seek a White House

Chain a trigger
Rope an elephant
Kiss a Cobra
Fight a Gorilla

Who are you kidding
When you're a dark horse
As if you're bidding
And gambling against the House

It's a loser's hand they say
Stakes too high
Pick 'em up and back away
For it could be do or die

Out front are the money players
Holding pat to hands of gold
Not even the Pope's prayers
Could force them to fold

Running up the polls
Taking down the competition
Most chasing the leaders paying their tolls
Chancing logic with reason

Thinking possibly just maybe
A fast dark horse
Could catch up on his own money
By engaging the Hispanic force

Build a fence
Make them pay
Never did make sense
Until he'd said he's doing it anyway

Dirty money, drug funding
Even the Clintons got clean
Before being caught under dunning
Allegations of the White Water scene

The Dark Horse pursues White House superiority
A beacon in the scenario
When the beam of the silent majority
Lit up his Sombrero

Mexico decided to step up
And play the big game
Rolling the dice into a cup
Of the Dark Horse with no name

Now running to and not from
Passing the faster horses on the rail
To fight the forces of the Kingdom
The Dark Horse pledged his tail

The race got close and mean
All the other horses ganged upon
The Dark Horses' Queen
Tearing her apart before dawn

She gave in to the masses
Exposing the Dark Horse to blight
No longer kicking asses
DH fell out of sight

The campaign came and went
DH rode in on the wind as a stag
Without the Party's consent
He held up the third party flag

No longer was it just
The red and the blue
It was another party thrust
Into something brand new

When the election was enforced
It was the White House
Needing the Dark Horse
To out run the rest of the course

The moral to this story is
Give the Donald a chance
To do his show biz
And he will win the Big Dance

So the Dark Horse can prance

THE WHITE HOUSE

Pennsylvania Avenue winds
As the sun shines
Towards the seat of power
A mortal spirit tower

Citizens support this throne
With votes alone
Hoping for humble leadership
With a just whip

Government is said to be in balance
Allegiance is the stance
Jeopardized by outside threats
Testing honor it begets

Branches there mostly theory
Much more than democracy
Its men asked to be more than self
With feelings on the shelf

President or Senator merely (wo)men
Born to die as we have been
But asked to assume our fate
By laws for land and State

Whether it be a white house
Or the shack in Foust
Men have declared their independence
To live free of immoral suspense

Could it be this right is abused
As to be heard is defused
By officials in secret chambers
Hidden from us voting members

Plato said of the price of freedom
That all want some
Regardless of the rational need
Dogs will even demand to breed

Orwell too predicted times of doom
As minds astute must loom
Squelching the simplicity of man
Until revolutionaries stand

Rome then Germany wrote the history
Of government by misery
Later we've read the immoral accounts
Of tactics we now renounce but pronounce

But have we learned our lesson
Or is man prone to treason
To principles based on declared right
With dollars wilting logic's might

No it appears people must weaken
To power of a rhetorical beacon
Aligning themselves to jobs and money
Ignoring goals of our country

So the White House up on Capitol Hill
Crumbles to a weakened will
By men's weakness to assert and compromise
Themselves to intellectual lies

As Polonius warned through Shakespeare
Yourself you must fear
For truth unto other self must be
Before life is honesty

Will this wrong ever be righted
Before our destiny is kited
So the majority is represented
And the power of money has been repented

Elections and selections
Fair and square of insurrections
Must be based on principles
With political partisans feigning disciples

While freedom and equality if any
Representing the Many
Defending the invincible crew
Against the dominant Few

While the White House defends you

THE COMMON CENTS OF IT ALL

The complexities of our world
The battles for flags unfurled
Is there simplicity there
That can explain
How to have happiness in spite of pain

Is it so hard to know
Not why but how to grow
Does it have to be deciphered
By the professors of Harvard and Yale
Turning the glow of life
To a confused pale

Why does it have to be so hard
Why is it scientific to have grass in the yard
Or success dependent upon the turning of a card
Nay that's only the human's way
Wanting to impress
To assume the power
And control the press

Rather than giving a simple yes
We pull it through the cloak of complexity
Watering it down with ingenuity
Until there's no such thing as purity
No such thing as the ease of an understandable truth
And the uncast shadow of youth

That merely assumes that we have to live through monsoons
And shouldn't have to control the weather
Or recreate the aerobics of a feather
It's not necessary to multiply divide and carry
For the sake of making it hard
Till jokers are wild holding the hole card

With common sense and good will
Lost to the complexity of nonsense and hell
While the soothsayers spout
And the intellectuals pout
About
Politics climate change terrorists
And all other indefinable events

By referring everything to an algorithm
Or an Evangelical hymn
To make sure once again
That a Trump card doesn't win

The other cards in the deck
Dumbing down the electorate
Making transparency after they inspect
And keeping public opinion in check
"Now look"
"It's an Issue not a probem"
"Now Listen here"
"It's God's will"
"Right to life"
"Right to choose"
"Black lives matter'
"White lives matter more"
"Prayer out of the schools"
"Debate away the country's fate"
"Free college tuition"
"Unlimited minimum wage"
"Maximum wage"
"Public officials are above reproach"
"The President's irresponsible"
"It's the media's fault"

What happened to common everyday
Horse sense
Gambled away
On dollars and nonsense
Oh for the forties and fifties when a dollar was gold
And patriotism never grew old

Purchased with good ole common cents

THAT SPECIAL BREED

Breed that steed they say
Maintain that stud and its blood line
For to quality they will pay
More for beauty than the horse's behind

Thoroughbred hybrid
Looking for the combination
Even people are wed
To changing God's natural selection

Do it better
Build it higher
Make it fatter
For the buyer

I wonder if
And wonder how
If God is good
Will he allow
Us to make wood
Out of a cow
Or a winning horse
Out of a losing course

What I'm saying
If you're listening
Might we not be delaying
By assuming personal Christening

So if you're that special breed
Number one seed
Of the potential few
I will come
To you

Tethered to your horseshoe
Committed to your breed
Honored to
Ride that special you

The stud of the triple few
Seattle Slew

MY YELLOW CONVERTIBLE

Growing up wishing on a star
Needing status with no sin
Wanting a cool car
Dads were different then

They had very little
In those hard times
Gone thru a depression
He tried to understand

I tried to be patient
He looked and found
He bargained… too high
He walked off without a sound
Disappointment future dim
Hurt I blamed him

Then destiny took hold
A car '50 Ford Ford beauty of my time
Came to Dad at a good price ($250 sold)
Like the color of a 1957 sunshine

And a sheen of hand lacquered paint
With a midnight top that sometime works
With a manual shift and looks of a saint
A mellow yellow convertible with fender skirts

My pride grew I was more
A gas fill-up at $.35 per gallon
$5 per month not too poor
I could ride a week on that stallion

As it drove into my life
I became full
Look at me
My car's beautiful
Hiding my insecurity

I even wore my glasses
And my hair blew
Look at me to the masses
As my yellow convertible flew

Now my son wants a car

And I told him my story
So he could wait and let me
Enjoy my yellow convertible glory
As I show him how to be

In a bargaining strategy

WARREN COUNTY FAIR

The Warren County line
The limits for wine and dine
Made up the boundaries
Fun for friends and adversaries

The harvest was in
Jack and Jill looked
For a thrill
All the girls were there
At the Warren County Fair

Looking for cooler boys
And stuffed animal toys
Coin tosses and rubber balls
Midway bosses among the horse stalls

For this we walked many miles
Hoping for a kiss amid the smiles
If you were shy to save face
It was the meeting place

For only the lonely
And find that one and only
Tent shows and games of chance
Along with girly shows and new romance

Of course for the boys
While 4H and city types made noise
It was all about the girls
In the clicks for chicks and tilt-a-whirls

A social order forming
With this carnival and barnstorming
Thrills and chills were a Joey Chitwood crash
Giving thrills to a small town bash

Looking back on those Fair Days
I'm trying to track my life through a phase
Marked by a small town County fair
With my slicked down hair

And low slung jeans to wear
Now that there is no time to spare
I wish I were back at the Warren County Fair
And my heart and lust just isn't there
For the Iowa State Fair

THE EDGE OF THE FOREST

THE EDGE OF THE FOREST

Standing on the tundra is a herd
Unmoving and alert
Above circles a scavenger bird
Moving and inert

Lying on the tundra is a pack
Creeping and poised
Behind following the predator's track
Are the litters hunger voiced

This is the drama of nature's balance
Wolf versus caribou
Backstage awaiting their entrance
The Ravens as the predators slew

This is the meticulous scheme of things
Where there is no beginning or end
Except the chase and the fear it brings
Until the kill or injuries mend

The chase begins and picks up speed
Run caribou run
The plot thickens will the wolf pack feed
Upon the stamina then done

A wolf is never alone in the hunt
A pack is to strike
But the Caribou is too quick far in front
And cunning hunger ends the like

As persistence is to stalk to seek
The scent is there
A wolf seeks out the weak
Set in motion to snare

The hunt may last for days
But the economy of the Artic is sure
To a ritual older than human ways
No pursuit ends in failure

So one on one it leaps
The wolf strikes a straggler
Only to lose its grip away it creeps
Blood is drawn senses stir

A sniff of blood is now the trail
Only one target the wounded
Inevitably doom comes to the frail
Ten seconds as death is sounded

After the neck is broken and hunger abated
Dependent scavengers stand in line
To fill their needs appetites sated
As wolves upon caribous they dine

To the herd the kill is merely an episode
They continue to move in time
Balanced is the system not to erode
Because the mothers are in prime

The stomping grounds are littered raw
With the calves a life is born
Into the immaculate natural law
Their instincts form future forlorn

Of age and winter descending
An urge to move is there
The herd starts again to sending
Themselves against the lair

Wolves and waiting predators seek the prey
Knowing they will come
Because it's meant to be that way
Nature's balance is not dumb

As the guardian of the species
For to the fittest will be strong
Without need for outside crises
Humans tag along

Until there crisis at the American boarder
On the hallowed ground of the grizzly
They and man bother the order
Until the system fails predictably

The herds and packs are depleted
Close to extinction
Causing wildlife to look defeated
Without distinction

Humans react almost too late
No fault is accepted
Blamed upon the quirks of fate
Reasons are emancipated then enunciated

Standing on the edge of the forest
We look with awe
Upon this miracle in which we've messed
Hoping to restore nature's law

Nature's law which has been forever
Passing before and after us
Relentlessly to be enforced despite endeavor
Never ending as we must

Believing this is standing with the maker
Accepting the balance
For ourselves and the caribou's predator
Survival is not by chance

No longer endangered are the caribou
Nor are the wolves forced south
Into the USA just down from Caribou
Lost to packs of wild coyotes or a dog's mouth

The sounds are back
Howling from the pack
While the caribou
Are alert to the threat coming too

Keeping the edge of the forest
In balance the sum of one wolf quest
Is to take two caribou to arrest
Too many of either they must digest

Then Natural Law will not divest
The survival of either's treasure chest

GIVE HER A CHANCE

Give her a chance to be great
Don't ask your mate to sit and wait
On the roost at home
When she also has the urge to fly and roam

The family unit yes it's divine
And raising children is the woman's incline
But I think us guys have to recognize
That she also is seeking life's full prize

She is asked to set down the roots
While he flies around to bring home the loots
He looks to her to be in her place
And guide him home from the rat race

She on the other hand may have a different idea
To dock the ship and calm the sea
For she wants him to understand priority
That for sure it's her responsibility

To clean the boots and mend the family lace
But she also wants to taste the air of outer space
Up where the sky is clear blue and rainbows start
And things look brand new and far apart

This is only natural and such
For a cinder in the pouch
Shall never be a pearl
Till that woman can still feel like a little girl

With the excitement and sensation
Of having some impact on creation
So you guys must recognize
That to let her fly up into your skies

Is to let her see the benefits of her plan
So diligently and on the other hand
It might not hurt for you to land
And see what it's like to stand

Upon the ground
With the fruits of your labor all around
While she can see how being home bound
Is the thrill of the love you've found

Yes by giving both a chance
To understand how being her will enhance
That such a flight is about being free
The ultimate romance being you being me

WELL HEALED

Well healed people have few problems it is said
Well healed people only have challenges
The healing already took place
Deep within their inner space

When they realized that simple unhappiness
Was disguised
Disguised as selfishness
Frustration hidden under the bread basket of loneliness

Of being withdrawn within one's self
Being the taker not the tooth fairy or Santa's elf
The healing if it happens
Must descend from the soul to the mind

And take the sacrifices of being behind
Being willing to turn the cheek
Being willing to scale and take a risk
To reach the proverbial peak

It takes simple yet profound
Acts of righteousness each day
That becomes the price the well healed
Must pay

Well healed in faith
Not fearful of the risk
As the kingdom comes
For those who are realists

And know the only way to be well healed
Is to plant each day good deeds
As the price to pay
For the harvest of the field

And the freedom one's wield
For the return yield
Of the well healed
From a shortcut repealed

For a moral letter sealed
And returned to the sender
As the vendor
Of those who render

Service to others is the recipient of the well healed

POTLATCH

(American Indian word of the northwest coast)

"An opulent ceremonial feast of health
At which possessions are given away
Or destroyed to display wealth
To enhance prestige and say"

The native tongue
Is so wise
It speaks to simplicity
It doesn't hide
Nor disguise
The essence of insecurity

It gets to the heart
It gets to the soul
Without being smart
Just being whole

Potlatch is one of those words
Simple in its meaning
Or haven't you heard
About tenderness of a mother's weaning

Kindness of a mother
To her newborn child
Apply it to one another
Humanity is reconciled

It's giving to receive
It's accepting without regret
It's not to deceive
What God has in His son beget

The choice is yours
Each day and with each person
In not just what you say
But acts without reason

So potlatch
In its simplest form
Is like the use of a match
To start a fire to keep us warn

It starts out small
Lifting others
Until they're tall
As hate and distrust smothers

If potlatch
Could touch us all
We could love
Instead of brawl

Peace on earth goodwill to men
Goodwill without sin
Is the goal of the majority
And the vestige of the minority

Why should the few rule
When we have the Yule
Where the pride
Is the purview of many nationwide

Is it for peace and space
In our neighborhoods
In our work place
In all of us getting out of the woods

So why should fear be war
That dictates our behavior
Corrupting our future core
To take it back from those that lack

Potlatch

So let the majority decide
And the terror will subside
Yes honoring those that died
But keep diligent against those that lied

Responsible tribal values are still America's pride

FREEDOM

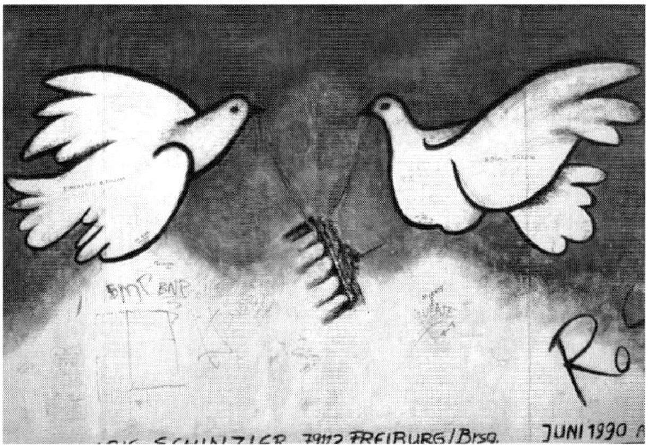

Freedom takes many forms
It's the bird flying its own way
It's the ship plotting its own course
It's the writer inscribing his thought
It's the lovers rolling in the hay
It's the success attained without force
It's the butterfly that's never caught

Freedom must weather many storms
Like the dingy upon the raging seas
Like the sleep that knows no dreams
Like the babe that is black of skin
Like the pod that has no peas
Like the mind that has no schemes
Like the fighter losing his will to win

Freedom must overcome manmade scorns
As the child who arrives unwanted
As the swan ugly to the eye
As the fool deaf and dumb as well
As the hero who becomes daunted
As the leader who must know the reason why
As the orator that has no spell

Freedom then must set the norms
In a system created by natural laws
In the minds of humane leadership
In the hearts of relentless peaceful men
In the veins of a mindful pause
In the soul of the mortal's grip
In the Judgment of repented sin

Freedom: this passion and love of life
That's passed to the newborns

FUTURE INHERITED

We inherit the wind
The world
The future

We inherit the genes
The personality traits
The facial characteristics
The voice texture
The goals and aspirations
Career selection

We inherit the family environment
The home structure
The locale and
Life style

We inherit the future or
Reject the wind
In your sails
At the home stead

Such as two brothers
One an alcoholic
The other a teetotaler
One unemployed
The other successful
Why didn't they inherit
The future and wind
That the storm assails

Aren't we either the victims
Or the beneficiary of the inheritance
Read this observance
It's the choice not the genes
That makes the difference

The good dad and mom
Make the right choices
Their offspring typically
The same choices
With the same voices
And sail through life

The bad dad and mom
Make the wrong choices
Their offspring typically follow
The same path
With the same wraith
And fail to a stormy life

Then we have the bad dad and mom
Giving their offspring the choice
Do I inherit the future
Or do I try to change the past
Or do I choose another path

The irony here is prophetic
We all can choose a path
Despite our past
Reject what we have learned
For what we have earned

To inherit the wind then yearned
Good or bad
Happy or sad
It's your life

SUPER BOWL MONDAY

Where will we go and what'll we do
When all is gone but a thrill or two

We race here and play there
Sometimes we forget to care

We hit the ball and drink the beer
We boo the ump then we cheer

We gather steam throughout the year
Awaiting Super Bowl week to appear

My God we're following the followers
Into that senseless mass of hollers

Can't we realize there's no prize
For mindless spectators of a staggering size

Making noise for their team of boys
Sunday after Sunday fewer simple joys

Culminating each year on Super Bowl Sunday
With bigger and bigger let downs on Super Bowl Monday

The losers weep and hope for more
And the winners become old hat and a bore

This present day tragedy gives us all highs and lows
Where it's leading no one knows

More than likely to be a social crash
Left among a rubble of gladiators and sour mash

This is history this is the way of man
Relieving themselves missing the marching band

Catch the thrills in your basketball sir
With little hope for a happy life following soccer

Forgetting how the flowers smell
Never singing but texting on your Cell

Listening to a commentator's words
Purchased with a ticket to the Redbirds

Now a symbol of nature's beauty
With shoulder pads and played for booty

Crowds have always gathered
When they thought it mattered

To a hanging or a rooster fight
Thrills were bought by black brown and white

But now this is a weekly affair
Foregoing church and the peace of prayer

Little time is spent
Together as families for what is meant

Alas this we'll certainly repent
In years to come to our moral decent

Like the Roman Gladiators
Demanding safe working theaters
With time off on Sunday
And equal pay

Unless we resurrect the simpler demands
Back to the art of the mind and hands

Playing music and the marches for the ears
Not just before the bowels and cheers

Then with our growing senses we can say
We have forgotten the blues today

On Super Bowl Monday

BON APPETITE

Lovin' is fun anytime
When you get the feeling
Morning noon or night is fine
Bon Appetite aren't you sweet

Had it for lunch
It's better than food
Morning's good but noon's too much
Bon Appetite aren't you discreet

Lovin' is feeling strong
When two become one
From sunup to sun is done
Bon Appetite aren't you one to meet

The thrill of lovin'
Beats any conventional meal
Try it for lunch
It's as natural as Sunday brunch
Bon Appetite aren't you more than a tweet

Lovin' is when the urge calls
Let it come
Get it together don't stall
Bon Appetite aren't you neat

Lovin' is a longing lust
When I have the chance
Anytime is good for a midday romance
Bon Appetite knocks me off my feet

So let's leave the food for the oven
And Bon Appetite for the Lovin'
Masseur and mademoiselle
Masseur and Masseur
Mademoiselle and Mademoiselle

Bon Appetite all is well

STATUS

I'm high on the hog
I'm the top of the totem pole
I'm the superstar
I'm the most valuable player
I'm very important
I'm a legend in my own time

Color them others green with envy

How high can status secure
How low can life be impure
When others look at the pasture
Not seeing the fame occur

Status climbing is like seeking
An endless mountain
There's no end for peaking
Once you drink from its fountain

Once you've attained
That certain height
It must be sustained
Like a windless kite

Holding yourself up there
Is quite a feat
Attaining God's chair
Blessing his seat

So seek your status
Above the clouds
Call yourself the upper crust
And look down upon the crowds

But watch out
Big shot
Failure is all about
Don't lose your hard earned spot

How high are you
How high can you get
Who's looking at your pasture
Everyone can be unsure

Since the future is impure
You aren't the sun or the moon
You only exist for a time
Don't be a victim of my rhyme

For the saying
What goes up must come down
May well resound
In your status reversal

And the crowd
You hadn't endowed
With gratitude
Will gladly celebrate your loss of altitude

HITTING THE RAILS

Trampled Troubadour
Strangled bedraggled
Lonesome lobo
Hopeless hobo

Chasing the train
Hitting the rails
Life of eating nails
Tipping the scales

Dead end trails
Empty milk pails
Lonely coyote wails
Torn down sails

If all else fails
Hit the rails
Storm and hails
Unclaimed mails

Heart that ails
For bread that stales
Hoisting fresh hay bales
Holding sweet females

As hope stops in jails
After hitting the rails
Oh Daddy
It's good to have you home
No longer do you have to roam

A HISTORY ON THE RUN

1931 32 33 my dad and his two brothers
Rode the rails during the depression of '29
No food at home
No hope for crops to hone
Boxcar knees
One meal a day please
Cold Coal rail cars
Long barrel shotguns battle scars
Illinoi Central Rock Island Line
No wine and dine
Lonely bums on the run
Cold back of the yards get down son
With warm camp fires
Railroad Dick with a stick that never tires
Trade coal for a meal
Just drunk enough to hide then steal
Earned a dollar per day
If farmer decided to pay
Or given a meal to stay
Hard time served or slave labor
Dirt poor had no money to savor
Life on the rails
Not for gals pals or snails
As hope stops in jails
After hitting the rails
Oh daddy George
It's good that you got home
No longer did you and your brothers have to roam

Dedicated to
George Leonard Rhoads, Wilbur Rhoads, Loren Rhoads
(20, 19 and 18 years old when they did it
Growing older by the hobo minute)

STILL WATERS

The flood settles into it resting place
Its torrents have ravaged the plains
Cutting paths like wrinkles on the earth's face
Created by storms and drenching rains

Like hysteria this phenomena comes and goes
Rising and falling on the chest of Father Time
Striking out against the calm as the wind blows
Threatening the very humility of man kind

As the flood waters seek out and find
The weaker ways sifting and shifting as it pushes by
Scattering hopes of brighter days
Leaving destroyed the security amid the cries

Calmness eventually overcomes its impatience
Gaining some control and feelings become rational
Cleansed... cleansed much as if the minds were rinsed
Stilling the waters on the skull and hull

Still waters run deep even in the minds of the victims
Who have to go on with their lives
Rebuilding their dreams
Despite the raging streams

Turned to oceans then the weather bested
As el nino dictates the future
With its power vested
By Mother Nature

To torture then reprieve its sons and daughters
With still waters

THIS IS NOT GOODBYE

Ups and downs bumps and stings
Life consists of all these things
Fighting for a place to lite
Hoping for a love that's right

When you find her it's a wonder
So don't lose her it's a blunder
If they move on as they must
Don't be cruel or unjust

Try to understand that life's that way
But the ties will not decay
Keep those memories for in time
A simple call will tie the line

This is the right cause we know
Touching people makes us grow
And once we stretch beyond our size
That's what makes a person wise

So don't say goodbye
Only to live the reasons why
Look and you shall find
Why lovers learn to spy

Why the new born babies cry
Why the flock stands nearby
Why Jesus was expected to die
Why the salmon always try

Why the good comes so high
Why because this is the way of mortals you and I
Why the seagull loves to climb
Destined to meet those that mark our time

Something real something prime
As deeper words expressed in my rhyme
That's why you keep it at any cost
This is friendship and it can't be lost

So this isn't goodbye
It's just hello to another why
Phone or call that's our deed
Why not be there when in need

Never too busy to keep in touch
Remembering those that mean so much
All this means is to believe the fate
Tomorrow is just another date

That's what brought our paths to cross
And that Maker won't stand the loss
For friends are forever
Up until the next to never

This is not goodbye
For the spirit we have will never die
It's kept in the casket only till we fly
As endless energy in God's eye

X
WHERE GOOD crosses BAD

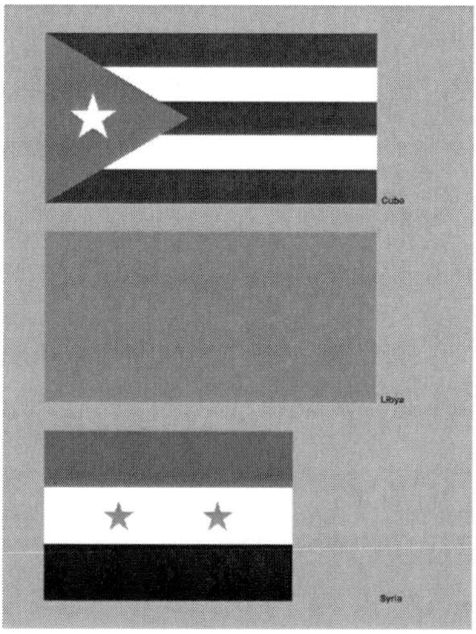

X MARKS THE SPOT WHERE GOOD crosses BAD

/ GOOD	BAD \
Love	Hate
Charity	Greed
Hope	Despair
Friendship	Enemies
Righteousness	Shallowness
Honesty	Deviates
Truth	Lies
Desire	Self-indulgence
Dedication	Inconsistency
Independence	Dependence
Sharing	Indulgence
Sexuality	Suppression
Positive	Negative
Success	Failure
Enthusiasm	Depression
God	Devil
Prosperity	Lavish

Are we good
Or are we bad
Check what the word's mean
Then do what we must
To do what we redeem
To be good

For being the other way
Is but to accept being bad
While forsaken weaknesses say
Words about being sad

As an upstanding human being
The good column is a challenge at any age
Living up to perfect isn't demeaning
And failure is not redeeming

But believe that to seek is to find

MY BEST FRIEND

Friend: a bond of mutual affection

You are my best friend
Many are trying to be
Many are trying to end
This tie between you and me

We've held each other
Overcoming doubts
Held between even sister and brother
And the word infatuation shouts

I love you
You're my best friend
So what could I do
If it were to end

For enemies hope we will slip
Unless we are hard and smart
Enemies of our friendship
Will fill the days we are apart

Hoping we don't need remedies
Being away from each other
Without lasting memories
Just as an indifferent brother

Always be my best friend
The one I've loved like no other
Never expecting it to end
Until the day comes together

To lay down with my best friend
And traverse on the eternal wind

RUNNING FROM LIFE

Are you running from life
Running away from dreams
Or trying to catch
Someone else's wife

To cut across rigid seams
Who never said
I'll buy tomorrow
Before I'm dead

And live in no sorrow
As a dreamer
As a schemer
As a social redeemer

Running after brothers
Chasing daughters
Looking to make friends
With all the others

But never growing up
Never able to pour
Life from my own cup
That now lies broken on the floor

Are you running from life
Running away from dreams
Caught in the chest with failure's knife
Killing all meaningful schemes

Becoming the death of hope
The death of a runner
Fallen upon the downhill slope
Into the grave of the dead tail gunner

Who ran out of room
To live longer
Because his mother's womb
Didn't give him the will to run stronger

When you hit the wall running from life
Stop and look back
At your life and your wife
Finally realizing you running on the wrong track

HOME STEAD

Home is so warm
Home is to keep away the storm
It enables you to stay
When you're away

While wishing on a lonely bed
You're going home instead
Where your happiness Is bred
And your love is fed

Home is a nest
Home is the best
It caresses you when you feel lonely
It comes from that feeling only

Wishing for no stranger to be mislead
About being home instead
For friends can admit
It's the companionship

That holds the thread
Until you're home instead
Husbands settle down
Wives don't dance around

For no romance
Is better than the chance
Until they're wed
Of losing the Home Stead

Take my hand
And call me husband
Don't make love in someone else's bed
For no thrill shall settle our dread

Nor will it make your heart bless
If I'm much less
For the last supper's bread
Is the Home instead

Making a landing site
Each holiday and Christmas White
For your offspring
Giving the background for carols you sing

To be birds of a feather
Bringing all together
For it's a family that builds a home
From roots to wings we roam

Secure in the surroundings
Embracing the subtle things
With love and happiness there
That shows we care

That life is more than being mislead
That roaming is better than the home stead
Finding once and for all
That seeking other shrews to crawl

In the bed you make is your last fall

FAMILY BY ANOTHER NAME

Why must mortals flock together
Why not be the extension of ourselves
Only looking for self-fulfillment
Ayn Rand sketches such a fantasy

This premise for satisfying
The inability to relate to
Others looms heavy
On society

The family unit is losing
To such individual pleasures
It culminates in a disregard
For parental responsibilities

As children looking for love
And attention aren't finding
Only selfish mothers and fathers
'No I don't have time"
"Go out and play"
"Go upstairs we are talking"
"Shut up and go to sleep"

Although this may be a reincarnation
Of a misspent childhood for
The parent and society
That places value on individuality
"Go you own way"
"Do your own thing"
"Get high and don't worry about tomorrow"
"If you don't love 'em leave 'em"

This is the inner conflict of individuals that
Builds until it explodes
It shatters and scatters lives
To the loneliness of themselves

Ironically in the end they eventually
Turn to the flock that will
Take them in for what they are
A commune of lost souls
A gang of no goals
A mercenary army of moles
That gave up the security
Of the family for life's trip
By themselves

This isn't the end of the story
It's the beginning of a tragedy
As this mode of human behavior spreads
The insecurity of a society spreads
The insecurity of a loss of values spreads
The realities of insecurity and
Impromptu communes are vested
In crime drugs loss of values and
Low feelings of no productivity
It creates nothing to promote
Faith and confidence
In the minds of humanity

The gang is surely for security
Missing at home or no home
Based on rules of survival
And those with power rule
The mercenary is surely for revenge
On memories at home or hating school
Based on rules of anger and retribution

Ironically the minds of these lonely people are
Only thinking of themselves
Today is their only reality
Yesterday is dead and gone
And tomorrow is something
They never thought of buying
With their faith in worthy efforts

Relentlessly the cycle as in all social systems
Will make its inevitable circle
We are now in the grinding
Turn of individuality heading
For the home stretch of tragic
Self-gratification once we are there
We will find as the prize
The need for the family as
It existed in the beginning
Thank God the
Cycle always begins again

Families come and go
But communities live and grow
Under the pressure of loneliness
And the desire to be blessed
By another love confessed
As it is realized that a commune
A gang
A mercenary army
Is the crudest form of a family

By another name

SEARCHING

Old drawers are full of new memories
If you take the time to measure
To paw through old times
To pull out that simple treasure

Searching through an old attic
You may come upon a simple pleasure
For the best things in life you lose
Are laying below old shoes

And someone else's book
Waiting for the searching hand
The searching heart to overlook
While hiding out as contraband

Searching takes a will to understand
To have the time to cast
Thinking back into the misty past
Digging out traces in bygone places

Is better than being blue
It could be that you'll find
By only thinking of no reason to
Something old and something new

For pulling together the waste
Becomes in vogue
Even in good taste
Once owned by some Rogue

Making up my mood
Cleaning up my act
With what I lost then found
Discarded to be exact

Even damaged egos
Can be restored
With some new clothes
To overcome being bored

Or ignored for old reasons
As that treasure is somewhat fickle
When making past decisions
Are from being in a pickle

So check out under the old bar
Your dirty clothes hamper
Your trunk in the car
Treasures really aren't to pamper

Like that lotto ticket
You threw away as declined
Without checking to claim it
May be a winner that I could find

God am I stupid or just blind

Then it's all-out panic
Looking everywhere near and far
Even searching in the attic
The garbage then the car

But why would I win when I don't
Lose my cool for my lost honey
Or have the volition to say I won't
When it may be funny money

Hoping that number is my shooting star
It's the image of a new car
Taking a vacation to something far
Searching the nearest bar

Having no luck as I drink up

DEEPER THOUGHT

Deeper thought than immediate understanding
Is poetry
Some say say it simple
But simply said doesn't stimulate the temple

The temple of thought demanding
The temple of deep understanding
Sacrificing the immediate simplicity of ABC
For the poet does want you to see

That it does take deeper thought
Under within deeper yet
To delve into the depths we've sought
To create an unsown seed to beget

A Shakespeare a Gibran a Thoreau
Poetic giants who attempt to conceive
That love's regret can bestow
Our need to receive when asked to believe

It's more than reality
It's more than what's instore
Apparent in the scenery
It's the very quest to explore

The inner core of evermore
The fertile seed of human greed
The climbing vine to its divine
The thoughts becoming yet another's weed

The reasons why humans wait
And why emotions held so dear
For those they say they hate
Pass away when they seem so near

It's all of these thoughts and attitudes demanding
Which are apparently misunderstood
As there is no immediate understanding
Of why they're bad or good

And why people are different
Why they're unstable
Why they become what they recent
Why they're unpredictable

That's the poet's challenge:

Without surgery of their vocabulary
Without the hand written word
Without deeper reading of a dictionary
Poetry would be absurd

And deeper thought would be lost to the wary

HOURGLASS

Though the bottom will never end
The amount of sand to last
As eternal life shall extend
By the turning of the hourglass

We do see and feel the erosion of age
The ages lo they slip away
They slip away like the sand in an hourglass
And money on pay day

How many seconds in a minute
Minutes in an hour
Hours in a day
Days in a week
Weeks in a month
Months in a year
Years in a decade
Decade in a life

From fore to aft
From top to bottom
From day to night
How many grains depict the erosion of Sodom

Boiled down to its basic ingredients
And a multitude of infinite relations
We mentally envision events
Oblivious of our systematic creations

The hourglass isn't the end token
For it's merely tipped to begin again
But simply spoken
A never ending flow of time will transcend

At its own pace so our mind can know
Infinity through the predetermined hourglass
The process is a function of life's flow
The flow that allows the sand to go fast

The more orderly the flow
The easier the process
Just wholly dependent though
That immortality is more than less

On blending the pressures brought to bear
As the sand expands its might
On the land as it rushes there
What an unpleasant sight

Based upon how much sand each will sow
The hourglass of life is just the same
Within the bottom of the tow
It's just the process we have to tame

It may not lengthen the time to hurry
At the proper pace
But without the pressures of worry
It certainly will brighten the clock's face

It seems the heart and the soul
Work together and not apart
On how many seconds are in our last minute
And how many more minutes are in our heart

How many hours in our worst day
In spite of despair and adversity
That can't delay… aging with its decay
Bearing out our past and future history

How many times have you wished you'd taken the time
To partake of the feast
Rather than devour
Those ghosts thought deceased

Deciding to broil instead of fry it
Taking on a healthy life style
Partaking in a better diet
With exercise as a way to smile

Then how many hours in your day staying young
How many days in your better week
How often have you wished you'd bitten your tongue
Instead with a biting wit we speak

How many healthier weeks have we misled
How many meaningful years in our decade
How many times have we said
"If only I had another day to trade"
How many decades in a centenarian's nook
How many centuries in the good book
How many times do you think historians will take a look
At how you handled that hourglass it took

The relentless drummer pouring through
To make your life a worthwhile rhyme
Will not be a concern to even you
If days and nights are just sands of time

A process we can't start anew
Just the flow so we can behold
As the sand slips through
Mortal reasons for growing old

And the bottom will never end
The amount of sand to last
As eternal life shall extend
By the turning of the hourglass

As energy in the windmill wizardry
Our ashes thrown there
Flowing like sand to eternity
As the hourglass is always fair

To those who turn
Seconds into hours
Hours into years
And tears into the cremation urn

With our ashes being the sand
Before we were ready to go there
That slipped through our mortal hand
Broken like the hour glass left bare

Whence the savior to repair

DOUBLE TROUBLE SEEING DOUBLE

Double trouble
Double bubble
Seeing double
Doubles on the run

Hallelujah Have to two ya
There's more than just the one

Like Edward Edwards
And Herman Hermans
There's more than words
To a name
First and last the same
That's the double trouble game

William Williams
Like Norman Normans
On the other hand
A double bubble brand
Double trouble
Doubles on the run

Samuel Samuels
And Daniel Daniels
Sing for your name
Until it's the same
And the sun
Jumps under the moon

For those double cats in the cradle
Are playing a pair and a ladle
So John Johnson
Can flow a bubble
Seeing double
Doubles on the run

Curt Curtis
Names won't hurt us
And sticks and stones
Won't hurt Jonas Jones
Double trouble
Doubles on the run

Catch is true
If catch is through
Catch is twenty-two
Catch me if can
Catch me for sure
Name Major Major Major Major
Double trouble
Seeing double

The Major Major's on the run
And this poem is meant to make fun
Of double bubble gum
And a double trouble bum

Ho hum
I glad it's done

Now you should think of some

A WORTHY THORN

The fairest rose isn't without thorns
A worthy thorn isn't without sweetness
The worthiness of a thorn
Is but in the beauty of the rose

Hallowed be the rose
That blooms fair
Above the thorns

Fairer yet be the rose
That blooms worthy
Above the thorns

A life despite a thorn can be the
Fairest sweetest rose worthy
Of all it is

A thorn in waiting
For the groom
The colorful bloom

May be painful
When touched
By the bride

Holding it in abeyance
As the infatuation
Has died

The fairest rose isn't without thorns
A worthy thorn isn't without horns
The worthiness of a thorn
Is but the scorn of the rose

Dying on the vine from an over dose
Of doubt to dispose
Of a lack of love

A rose of any other name is pain

SCALES

Who says lady justice is never at a loss
Though blind folded and anointed
For the scales of the righteous
She should never be exploited

Tipped and tattered
Laws and morals scattered
To the far corners of what once mattered
She's banged and battered

Scales of snakes thus dampen
For the skins of bait
Truth can't just happen
Nor can it wait

For without this check to see it true
And for what has and should have been
Colors red could turn blue
The laws of nature must prevail again

Scales of justice
Its ignorance of both past and present
Has near crushed us
Against each other we resent

And towards ourselves
Liars and cheaters
Line the morgue's shelves
Society restrained as wife beaters

And saddened when they go
For they never learn to tame
What most don't know
That truth and love are one and the same

For truth to yourself is where justice came
To balance the scales
And then it can be done
As one and all prevails

And for whom the scales toll
Though tipped it doesn't bust
Ensuring life's justice for all
For truth makes the Lady just

Amen

SLEEPING ALONE

There was a time
The bed had two
Now there's but one
With the loss of you know who

You sometimes cry
When he's away
Asking God
Why he went astray

Time has told
Its bitter truth
You can't hold
This man searching for youth

Your bed may be empty
For this point in time
But you know someday
The sun will shine

Whoever takes his place
Let it be a man of worth
One that will cherish you
Above heaven and earth

For it's your heart
You must imbibe
Get the horse before the cart
So your interests will jibe

It's never just the sex
Or the bodies making love
It's the feelings for what's next
Each day fitting like a glove

With no sleeping alone
In a bed built for two
Now that you're the one
Loving him loving you

NEVER LOOK BACK

Never look back
Don't look over your shoulder pack
To see where you're going to
If your destination is in front of you

Look on down the road
Because you're carrying a heavy load
Don't look back
For all you'll see

Is a crooked track
Misgivings and muddled fact
Doubt and regret
Mistakes and retakes

Are in that sunset
Don't look back
Keep your eye on your destination
And believe that when you get there

There will be an elation
Not regret
In the goals you've set
Move on down the line

Be observant
But don't stop at every sign
Because the road may have an incline
And may beckon you to park along the way

But all I can say
Don't look back
For all you'll see is what used to be
What you thought you should have done

And why initiative doesn't end with the setting sun

Or battles you should have won
Or marathons you should have run
But failed to act
And it's a fact

You can't redo that track
So don't look back
Bridges are built
And mountains are scaled

By mortals like you
Who have failed
But have tried again
Because they never looked back

Where they've been
They just looked ahead at the challenge
Taking revenge against the obstacles
In their way

Holding doubts at bay
For in taking this risk
They display the faith
In why we exist

And why we must weigh
The acts of each and every day
Without looking back
We take it upon ourselves

To act
Then react
To life's attack
But never retract

Fact… never look back

LIFE IN A TENT

Stop for awhile
Peeks for a dollar
Close your eyes
Before you holler

They call me Rosa
The stripper
Loose as a goose
With my zipper

Take a look
I'm your fantasy
More than
Any lady can be

Hold me
In your eyes
Take a peek
Before the illusion dies

I dance I got rhythm
What a shape
Ask no more
Just shut up and gape

Love is out of sight
And out of mind
Take a peek
Unless you're blind

This the ode
To a life misspent
A life that's lost
In this damn ole tent

Just to pay my bills
And my rent
Waiting for the right shill
Before I repent

There has to be someone
Who will like me for me
Whether it be a father or his son
To set me free

From the oldest profession in history

MY LOVE WALKED ON

My love walked on
And my life stood still
Good times are gone
With this loneliness to fill

How could I let her go like that
How could I agree to see her go
Head and shoulders
Toe to toe

We went together

Like a water flow
The current was swift
And it was deep
I could even feel her
In my sleep

But my love has walked on

As I'm standing still
Not wanting to admit
She's gone
But dull for the aching thrill
Of her embrace

Her sweet smiling face

Are nothing but a memory
Walking on away from me
Lord how will I ever know again
When all I see is the way it's been

Regret you bet

Penance for sure
Searching for resurrection
Is all I can dare
But of course reality done
We are no longer a pair

So as the birds and bees are
And shoes and socks are
When lovers aren't it
And the shoe doesn't fit
You must wear it

And Walk On

RECEIVING CAN YOU GIVE

Reaching out has two meanings
You are either giving or receiving
In life we do both but with
Some it's receiving by deceiving

I like to think I give to receive
Without deception
But I wonder why I give
When others take exception

Principles and ideals are fine
They make you feel good
But is it a better life
By bending when you think you should

I wonder if I could live that way
Pleasing just myself each day
For the sake of anything
Taking without giving my selfishness away

No from the faces I see
Of those takers on the run
I feel good about my way
I can smile when it's being done

As for those takers justifying their case
They pay the final price
With loneliness
And graves of ice

Who shall remember Hitler for himself
He took from mankind
Without giving in his name to peace
Leaving shame and hate behind

Who shall forget Jesus for himself
He gave his life for mankind
Without asking why
He let the takers ease their mind

What is better is the question
To receive for your gifts
Or just take the gifts for yourself
Ignoring what good it befits

You have a choice my friend
It's ultimately left up to you
But remember towards the end
Your heritage will be held true

As your offspring follow you
Emulate you
Defend you
Give to receive as you do

Remember givers are deserving takers too

MEET THE CHALLENGE

Meet the challenge
Meet the opportunity
Meet the Maker
Avoid the undertaker

Mental spiritual and physical
When they're at one
The being is at peace
It can seek fulfillment

And meet the challenge
Then meet the opportunity
It can feel good in the morning
It can feel worthy during the day

It can feel fulfilled at night
It's not a climax
It's not a breaking of the dawn
And the setting of the sun

It's the continuation of the being
Never being done
Mental the spiritual and the physical
Are a being of one

No landslide no earthquake
No storm can take away
The challenge or the opportunity
For they are at oneness

Bred together
By the ultimate discipline
Of the mind the body and the spirit
This Karma is the heaven

Where the head and mind
Are at one
And the body and spirit
Meet the holy one

This is Dharma's answer to overcoming fear
By meeting the challenge
Filling the page
With meditation of a Sage

Letting yourself out of doubts cage

I THEE WED

To thee I wed
I said
I do
My love is you

Take me
Hold me
Say I do
And decree
It's always me

The word
You've heard
Spoken from my heart
Means we'll never part
As the rose and tart

Marriage is our bond
Joined by love oh so fond
Never to be separated
Nor alone we've hated
Not to be abated

Vows of love and charity
Joined as one are we
Us two then three
Children become our trinity
Then the family tree

This is our commitment
Given without resentment
No sacrifice too much
As told by our touch
Each other being the crutch

Kneeling we contemplate
Our fate
Ourselves each other
Our Father Mother
And one another

For richer or poorer
The rings create
A tithe of faith
Before it's too late
I can't wait

In each other we will trust
The meaning is for us
With others set aside
Until we've finally died
Thus do us part

For to make these sounds
Will quell our ups and downs
As God surely knows
Why together a human grows
As the everlasting has arose

Our sanctity our morals stand
Stroked by gentle hand
Growing into a bloom
And joined by a loving womb
Through dreams that stand

To fill spaces
With warm embraces
Take my hand
The wedding band
And say

Take me
Hold me
Say I do
And decree
It's me for you

For richer
For poorer
In sickness
And in health
I thee wed

Now take me to bed

THE CIRCUS

THE CIRCUS

The circus called to real life is in town
Jugglers high wire artists and the clown
Performing what we call the impossible feat
All stepping to the irresistible beat

Said to be today's gladiators who compete
Competing for society's attention
Much like a bad seed with deceit
And melt away the icy grip of apprehension

High wires and low cut attires
Midway and the fat lady
Races faces and turning aces
Grandstands and dealer's fast hands

It's the romance of the games of chance
As white horses prance
The sexy riders take the crowd's glance
While the elephants try to dance

The circus is fulfillment
Yes indeed thrills abound
It can grab you by the fancy event
To calm you down

If you like a fantasy
The three rings denote the Trinity
The Father the son and dreams to me
Though the Ghost may enter reality

Riding on a Stag
Carrying the American Flag
Holding out the goodies in a bag
For the kiddies to catch and snag

From the riders on performing horses in action
It's another example of illusions
A show entertaining as a distraction
From the problems of life's intrusions

Setting the stage with lions out of the cage
While other trained animals clamor around
We can smile at the reclusion of rage
As music makes the robust sound

The circus isn't competition to see who can win
It's entertaining yet not demeaning
For any reality or past sin
To those that need redeeming

From their bedtime prayers
When the show is finally done
And the love of prancing mares
Leaves the Ringmaster as the lonely one

Connecting the Father and the Son
With answers about the imagery and size
Though mere imagery is their fun
It delivers a subtle message in disguise

That the Circus isn't just for a first prize
But entertaining for all eyes

LISTEN OR LEARN

Listen or learn just do it
Don't try it
Don't fry it
Don't stew it

Don't marinate or procrastinate
For time won't wait on fate
Just do it
Listen learn through it

Don't age it or brew it
Just get to it
And do it
Climb out of your pit

Fried and alkalized
Because of a sensitive pride
The opportunity died
Listen learn do it

Don't make it
Don't fake it
Just take it
Upon yourself
No one else will do it

Listen learn get to it
Because if you don't
There's no blame to be had
It's really not sad or bad

So few do it
Because they never get around to it
And you'll be in the minority
By not treating sex as romance

For those who perform the puppet dance
And curse love as a circumstance
Afraid to take a chance
Impaled on their own lance

Trying to avoid their concern
Without the meaning of a caress
Because they didn't listen or learn
How to just do it without distress

With a Loving life and wife
In the pursuit of happiness

SANDBOX

Grain by grain
It has been poured
Day by day
It's been stored

But if it's cast
And turns to stone
No longer can seek its level
Nor will it stand alone

It will run and it will crumble
Time will come when feet will stumble
In its wake the past is sure to take
Visons through the hour glass bubble

Hour by hour
Like seconds
Time will devour
As destiny beckons

All can be well though not seen
Fine and smooth
Against the sides and back again
Flattened and hardened by the tide to move

Sliding to and fro the shore does fetter
Returning to where the surf's been
Knee deep in fish bones might be better
As if it hadn't bothered to go again

But nothing can be much wetter
Than those who sit together in the sandbox
Shifting sand in stormy weather
Counseling as sheep and the fox

Figures in the midst of a shower
Trudging through the wet sand
Then up pops a flower
I take it in my hand

But lo I can't understand
Why its beauty will wilt
Once I remove it
From the silt

I would think it needs more than sand
Fear not oh hands of cloth I stole
With humanity close at hand
And the flag curled around the pole

I shan't bring down a country
To my little old sandbox
Without some assurance perfunctory
Of the sheep and fox

That a patriot opens the locks
A crowd can gather around
And as he does enters the fox
Thinking maybe the world heard the sound

Of the children in this stormy weather
Playing in the sand
Are concerned about whether
Skylab will land

Or whether Syria should stand
They just talk of taking turns
Or Obama is qualified to command
Smiling and filling their urns

With the granules of the earth
And when it does and it may arise
To feed their joy and sooth their mirth
A child throws sand in another's eyes

The rest in unison rise
And justice be done
Without disguise
In tranquility all as one

The sandbox is strong and thrives
With no intrusions from the bigger jocks
As the rest of society denies
Mama buy me a sandbox

For a simple judgement of guilt
Is more cunning than the fox
If there are problems in the silt
Brewing from the sheep in the sandbox

When we have a God to protect the flocks

PUFF AND I'M GONE

So temporary
So lovely
So fragile
Nature ah what a peaceful symphony

A puff of dandelion
A puff of smoke
A puff of cotton
A puff of snow flakes

Help me I implore
Lest I blow away
As I struggle in your hand
Don't blow me away let me stay

Cause like the swirling sand
I don't restore
Help me I implore
Take your puff in command

Hold me close
And save me for my safety
If not the wind will shatter
My perfect symmetry
And my life will scatter

So hold this pose
Like you would with a fragile rose
Despite the thorns
With a heavy heart that mourns

Puff away

But pick me for your lover
Put me in your quiver
Pass me to lost then found
Save me from that wind's shiver

Then hold my blossom close
So final
So unfair
So blow away if you dare

Puff I will be gone forever into the air

MELTING RAIN

Ice can be treacherous
Ice can be chaos
Ice is never nice
Unless it is killing lice or mice

The rain falls upon the fertile ground
Accepting it as nature is profound
Be it dry or be it cold
It has life in its fold

Gently the river runs away from me
In its rush to the sea
Then as if willed the change of season
Stops it for no reason

As the temp goes down
To the degree 32
In changing the rain
From free to freezing glue

Frozen is its purpose
Then the sun comes upon the scene
Clinging to the changing surface
Glowing warm and serene

As the rays penetrate the air
It moves the rain from me to there
Rain… rain gentle care
Melting rain ground is bare

Slippery ice no longer there
Imposing broken bones
Composing sliding cars
Ice cream and frozen candy bars

Are the only remaining ice bizarre

SIESTA MOTEL

Jack and Jill
Looking for a thrill
Doing show and tell
At the Siesta Motel

Aren't they good
Aren't you bad
Just misunderstood
Rather than sad

Gambled for a penny
Lost for a buck
That's the pair out of luck
Making love out of muck

They couldn't make it
They couldn't fake it
After a short spell
At the Siesta Motel

Romeo and Juliet
Glad that they met
Doing show and tell
At the Siesta Motel

But they were fine
They were real
They made love
They didn't steal

Gambled for a promise
Won for a vow
Held together
Forever and now

Married to each other
Maiden unto a mother
Having sons for a brother
And all is well

Since their married affair
At the Siesta Motel

BEDROOM EYES

Looking down
Then looking up
As you look through my ceiling
I get this uneasy feeling

I guess I'm wise
To those bedroom eyes
Hide me in your stare
Let me be aware

That you really care
With that pair
Of bedroom eyes
Be they green
Or be they blue
Those eyes will tell on you

Loving is no secret
To be kept
Ever since our eyes first met
My heart's been set
On the prize
Behind your bedroom eyes

But you look away
About the time I want to say
I love you all the way
And it isn't the back of your head
That I thee wed
Nor will share my bed

So shift those bedroom eyes
Into my stare
Packaged as the prize
Making us a pair

Per chance you can't
Or want to play hard to get
Remember fools don't plant
Bedroom eyes on my corvette

Nor do they get
My heart to set
For it's a bet
Your bedroom eyes have gone wet

ON STANDBY

Air time
On standby
Slow time
Drags by

Met and spoke
Coffee cup
Conversation awoke
Picks up

More alike
Than not
Similar interests
That's what

Time dies
Tick tock
No disguise
Left to small talk

Passing time
To relax
Thoughts rhyme
Artifacts aren't facts

Nice time
Standby
Air borne
Clear sky

Nice to fly
After meeting
Someone
On Standby

Until it's a curse
That the someone
Is talking her verse
Ignoring me and everyone

Taking the last seat
Despite my plea
About home and family
Left to more time to meet
Another on standby
Just ahead of me

THE TIME HAS COME

My feeling is the time has come
I've been hiding and I've had to run
Though not deaf and I'm not dumb
I can't sing but I can hum

"I shivered at night
And sweated in the sun
Sipped the liquor
And never touched a gun"

I've talked of doing it
I've swallowed my pride
I've stopped the swing
So I could slide

Maybe my life is truly deaf and dumb
And maybe I could sing
If I forgot the tune to hum
Then took back the swing

And admitted to myself
The time had come
The time to recognize
That my prize would be twice its size

If I were to lower the level of my expected skies
Take it a little more easy
Put my nose to the wind when it's breezy
And sit back and relax when I'm feeling queasy

But though it may sound crazy
Only tomorrow isn't the least big hazy
When you're a fan as a mortal man
And think the Cubs can

Then believing is taking a risk
Upon the hand you kissed
Put your faith in the lone command
And you shall arise to stand

In Kingdom come
For thy will be done
By passing judgement
The time has come and went

For history is not deaf and dumb
With the words to sing and tunes to hum
Suckling's upon the thumb
Of Kingdom come

Singing fe fi fo fum
The time has come
For singers to sing among
The dead ringers to hum

Do Run Do run

DOESN'T MATTER NONE

Tell me what you've done son
But I don't know that it'll matter none
Come on pass it by me
Just for fun ignore the gun

Tell me what you've done son
Not that'll matter none
But there's no way
That I'm gonna put down this gun

So you'd better tell me for God's sake
What you've done son
Come on I'm not that bad Dad
Some indiscretions and mistakes
I've made and the setbacks I've had

All I can say is I'm sad Dad
Making circumstances look bad
That you had no reason to be glad
And what really makes me mad

Is that I tried to get help
For the sake of righting myself
And gosh it's really sad Dad
That now you think I'm bad

Come on son I know you're nervous
About this gun
But your life is just lived for fun
And even though it may be done

Here's your choice under this forgiving sun
And even though you might have the urge to run
Don't try to outrun this gun
And son if your virtues are re-won

Over what has just been done
And you can hold it in your heart instead
Then maybe you can unload this gun
So it'll never again be held to your head

Perchance you have the urge to run
Tell me what you've done son
Not that it'll matter none
But if you don't

The devil surely will have won
Well Dad if you really want to know
Look in that mirror when we are done
And you'll see I'm just my father's son

So hand over that gun
Before you decide to run
But you can't hide
From the truth of your selfish pride

That your son is you on the inside

NO ORDINARY MEN

Einstein Plato Socrates
They were men of thought

Franklin Jefferson and Lincoln
They were men of peace

Moses John and Jesus
They were men of faith

Elvis Sinatra and Bach
They were men of music

King Longfellow and Shakespeare
They were men of literature

Macarthur Churchill and Patton
They were men of war

Regan Kennedy and Clinton
They were political salesmen

No ordinary men were they

God created us and them to be
As much as we can be

He or she didn't create us equal
Only created us to be equal

His blessing is in each person's heart
And warmed with the spirit thou art

No ordinary man or woman
No discrimination meant

This is the beginning for us all
But the endings are far... far apart

To which we become
No incrimination consent

The reasons are down deep
In the thoughts we keep

Emanating from our desire
To go to sleep or set the fire

The makers and the doers
Become the pursuers
As the spiritual message allures

The takers and the breakers
No distinction intent

In many numbers
Can't appreciate their blunders

Destined they are the ordinary men
No discrimination intent

In this subliminal plan
Man and woman are given the upper hand

To do with as he or she sees fit
Using or abusing his or her mental wit

The tools are there that God
Is giving put in our map

To use for the living
No separation or gender gap

The mind that wants more
Is but a tool fertile and used except by fool

The ordinary man or woman envision
Accepting no civil rights violation

For to waste is worse yet
By foregoing what there is to get

For it's there you see
It's within us all you and me
All you must do
Is set it free
And then an extra ordinary man or woman art thee

Closing thought
Differences arise from the beginning toward the ending sequel
Born equal is not the same as born free to be equal

SOMEDAY MORNING

On a Someday morning I'll be happy
Someday afternoon I won't be blue
Someday evening I'll know what to say
For someday will be brand new

As the night time moon
Someday is in tune
Put off today's gloom
For tomorrow does loom

Avoid reality and high noon
Leave it to someday begotten
It won't hurt so much
When all is forgotten

Except the presence of today's ice
When someday morning's sun doesn't rise
And lightning strikes twice
Realizing why a liar lies

Someday relieves the scorning
And renews the yearning
For tomorrow's hopes are for Sunday's mourning
As yesterday's forgotten much less concerning

Well laid plans for Someday Morning
While singing and playing to the beat
When well-meaning is burning
We find ourselves in fast retreat

Singing "On a someday morning
In the afternoon
Reality can't make it
It's just too soon"

But in the someday evening
As we begin to sleep
Those someday dream's meaning
Is left to counting sheep

It has to be today's first call
So that spring hasn't turned to fall
And summer doesn't stall
Under a hard winter's pall

And for destiny to be believed
Climbing to the top of the mountain
So deception can be relieved
Becomes someday morning's fountain

The good life must be lived our way
Not someday

LOVINGTOWN

Passing down that road of haste
Ungluing this life of paste
I pass by and in my car
It was neither near or far

Just on this side of Decatur
Not much to be seen to occur
A quiet place with too few people
Just a few pets and that church steeple

With a small sign outside of town
Broken and falling down
Its name was singing
And this morning the bell was ringing

Lovingtown is there
Sending messages through the air
Come to my breast
A child and lover request

Keeping feelings in your chest
In front of the lust for life
So you can have the time to invest
In the value of a loving wife

Bumble bees and humming birds hover
And the meaning of history we'll uncover
For Lovingtown is a heritage
Alluring to all no matter age

Despite their wage
Holding services upon the stage
With true love as it's rage
Lovingtown is the turning page

Where you're able to impart
To those shallow hearts
Why it's so lonely
The likes of Lovingtown only

Passing down that road of haste
Ungluing this life of paste
I pass by this sign confronting my day
The Lovingtown sign trying to say

Live your life in the small town way

A DAY IN THE LIFE

A day in the life of a dreamer
Is like casting a net upon a stormy sea
An idealist and an emotional schemer
Just perchance what the catch shall be

For there shall be no guarantee
Nor reception of the metaphor
That a soul who only thinks of me
Can be playing the life of an actor

First writing the script designs
The laying of the plot
Then being equipped to draw the lines
From dot to dot

Thusly setting down the frame
Keeping it in the natural balance
For those dreams ideals and sweet refrain
For just the sake of romance

Galileo had to make this judgment
And Einstein later cleared the air
Of the likelihood of why dissent
To reality isn't really there

But yet it's gone with the passing of dawn
A day in the life of the mortal dreamer
Unless you understand that time is never gone
Is the idealist whose hopes shall the schemer

And the redeemer who can't hear redemption's call
Should listen for the curve
And observe the speed of its fall
As speed is the ultimate Master we serve

And by being too idealistic
Too erstwhile to the emotional Master
To serve the vital statistic
Shall lead the hypothetical to a floundering disaster

For they shall go nowhere
And as the history books dare
They shall not sincerely care
For to now their attitudes are unfair

As light's speed is the tool
To this other dimension and is time's wench
For reaching life's everlasting rule
With EMC2 theory of relativity is common sense

And direction that a continuum can fuel
Ah yes it is the day in the life of a teacher
Solidly reaching the minds of any fool
That time travel is the preacher

To teach us the ultimate benefits
Of settling religion's strife
That shall set down the testaments
The principles of after life

Not a big bang in the atmosphere
Not evolution's reality being fear
Not some far off being not even there
But the quantum of our being here

With our forbearer's belief near
By knowing how
A day in the life
Is putting the horse in front of fear
And the plow

As Eternity is forever not now

WHO LIES HERE

Back among the willow trees
Up on Red Dog hill
Exposed to the breeze
Is that country cemetery
With headstones quite contrary

Who lies here
Just outside of Toledo
That is two miles near
Is it the pioneers
Who overcame
The mountains and the fears

Those souls to keep
In their final stations
Fire sticks kill the bones
But the headstones
Are two miles nearer confessions

For a country to tame
Or is it their heirs
Who mated in pairs
Brave but unawares
Climbing heaven's stairs

Raising a family
In a free country
Or is it just a sign of the yesteryears
And the foundation for building today's careers
Burying our peers

Representing inspirations
And the heritage
Of strong nations
Who lies here
In their final stations
Just outside Toledo
That is two miles nearer
The last confessions

Most likely if you remove the headstones
And sift the dust
Which were once the bones
Of the just and unjust
You would find the true answers to existence
Left behind as the marrow of the past tense

The passing of a yesteryear
Resting in peace
Under the headstones of war
That never cease
And the answers to forever more
Which with dust to dust
Their demise has thus been marked

Now who lies here
Just outside of Toledo
With souls to keep
In their final stations
Fire sticks kill the bones
But the headstones
Covered with a nations sod
Turned to dust
Are two miles nearer God

THEY MISTOOK

They mistook this man
This shallow picture
This man of reprimand
I too mistook his Accenture

His character's intention
And his dimension
And felt that he was sincere
And held certain principles somewhat dear

But undeniably true
He could not act as he said he'd do
His words were shallow
His acts were fallow

His behavior told on him
He wanted to take the easy way and skim
So a depth I thought was his command
Melted upon the stand

Like so much carbonated fizz
Guess I mistook this man
I mistook his impatience as show biz
With the people at his demand

I mistook his word
His seemingly dedication became absurd
When he was asked to make the sacrifice
Heretofore he turned on those holding the dice

With his puppet strings
Whom he had held by the toes
Calling them stupid and ding-a-lings
For he was still trying to play his pose

As they hung him from the deck
I mistook his look
I mistook his intellect
Yes I mistook this crook

I thought if the glove fits
You must convict
Unfortunately it was a skit
And they did acquit

They mistook his behavior to be learned
And now that the boomerang has returned
He is paying for those he burned
Caught he wasn't even concerned

About brutal but true justice
With the no repentance of prejudice
To me and now for all see
We mistook a monster for a man of dignity

If you know this deviate
Let me know
For whom we all have met
And almost let him go

O. J. Simpson
That so and so
Also
Bernie Madoff
Osama bin Laden
Adolph Hitler
Joseph Stalin
Judas Iscariot

At the table of the last supper a Jesus foe
No O. J. but history will know

I CAN FLY

I CAN FLY

True compassion
Is knowing when to help what to say
It's the capture of emotion
And how to light a cloudy day

Keeping sorrow and despair
As sunshine can melt the fog
Away from the morrow of ill repair
And a hearty axe can hew the log

The true act of compassion
Isn't the tears and the gentle hug
But more likely a plan
To get your spirit from under the rug

A compassionate friend
Can take you by the chin
Lift your head then
Convince you to win

By just telling you
How great it's to be alive
What a miracle you are to
Be what nature did contrive

To be emotionally free
And that each day is a new life
To pare away emotional obesity
Delivered by a loving midwife

Whose compassion is an act
Of looking another in the eye
And outlining the fact
That only birds can fly in the sky

Until man decided that he must fly
Putting his mind to wings
And his mind to work or die
And his ingenuity that belief brings

The joy of accomplishment
And a total mental repair
Through subtle attainment
Of an aimless life in despair

To get the unpassionate to believe in it
With the courage
And compassion of being mentally fit
Just keep turning the page

And finally just do it
SAYING EVEN I CAN FLY
TODAY IS THE DAY
GIVE ME A WAY

Just like the Wright Brothers did it

THE MENTALITY OF LOVE

Yes the mentality of love
Is set in the minds of very few
Though on the minds of many
Who want to just try it with you

Raising one's spirit through the involvement
And intimacy of another
The soft downy feel of a feather
And the earnest protection of a tether

Cradled in the arms of security
With no other who shall know me
More than you do to remove
The fruit upon my tree of love

It's what all humans are pining for
But most don't know how to imply it
They take the easy way to open the door
And just want to try it

They try to fake it
They try to make it
But its undeniably true
That the heart the soul the mind
And the body too

Must activate a sense of permanence
Much like the emotions
Exemplified by the Nativity
With that feeling for another

As earnest as the safety of a mother
And lo this isn't easy for "him" to see
It takes an immense amount of humility
Sacrifice and willingness to make more than money

It may take an effort to entice
The trust and commitment as the price
So it's as soft as a feather
And as firm as burnished leather

And so inclined to sincerely mean
I love you for all you've been
So long as you can be
What my mother was to me

Will this trial run really work
Does it take the mystery out of bedding
Making you feel it's your worth
He wants not the wedding

The dance of the dinosaurs
May commence in earnest
With sex drive in his drawers
While attempting to prove he's the best

Yes the mentality of love
Is set in the minds of very few
Though on the minds of many
Who want to just try it with you

Imagine even if it will pay
To put off discussing the wedding day
And you're not just another lay
The mentality must not be put on delay

If you're ever going to have love your way

FRECKLES

Speckles upon the egg
Rain upon the window pane
Sand upon the sea shore
Aren't the freckles much more

On you they are
That lovely sign
Of sunshine
They're set to glow
As you smile

Glistening all the while

Twinkling below your eyes
Like stars behind the cloudy skies
Catching tears from the cries
As emotions rise

I love those spots
Of brown and gold
Fortunes told
With cheeks ablaze
I must amaze
At your lovely eyes and ways

Let's not lose those freckle days

They're so few
Without you
My former freckles would
Turn blue

Now so pale
Not having gone to Yale
Or on accord from Harvard
My looks are stale

Until I look at you
As freckles seem to prove
That what you say is true
Those cute spots certainly move

Us to admire your groves
As happy to singing the blues
Above all things to choose
Freckles are your natural tattoos

NO ONE KNOWS

No one knows
It comes and goes
It's behind your eyes
And beyond your nose

That you truly do love me
That most can't see
As it comes and goes
So no one really knows

Having me the way you do
The way you can
Most everyone else
Is just guessing rather than

Trying to understand
Love when your temper blows
Intermittent until no one knows
As fighting just comes and goes

With humility showing no foes
Secrets are for those
Telling the truth with the language
Of their body's pose

And can't live reality
So as you look at me
So no one knows
That your temper comes and goes

Like trees are planted in rows
As I manage a smile all the while
I will know you do beguile
My whimper that comes and goes

It's just nature's way of expressing
What we can't say
Though our actions betray
A real love can have a bad day

So our real intentions
Show in how we pose
Move our eyes
And read this prose

Leaving doubts to our foes
And the twinkles to our toes

EATING WITH THE CROWS

When the grain is upon the ground
And you're hungry
Do you look around
Do you see

Do you take it for what it's worth
Without asking
About its origin about its birth
As you need to break the fasting

If you step back for a second
To test the air
Despite your desire as hunger beckons
You really care

For then you know
For goodness sake
With no crow
Will you partake

Praise the primate danger
Slay the scavenger
Know the source
Limit the first course

For eating with the crows
Lowers our values
Even as the ground squirrels knows
That the food is not to confuse or lose

Hunger versus consumption

Overeating is a plague
Facing American's as they use
The food source as if to beg
The right to abuse

Only the scavengers overeat
For their survival
Since the time between meals
Is subject to revival

But obesity isn't for survival
Fighting for the right to overeat
Their health wealth and revival
Will most certainly deplete
Self-respect lost to self-indulgence

THE GOOD EARTH

Ashes to ashes
Dust to dust
From the good earth
Comes birth
In conception's worth
Laughing at a mortal's girth

Ashes to ashes
Dust to dust
No man shall perish
But perish he must
Unless he believes
That what God does is just

As the cycle of the good earth
As you turn the soil
And senses come to a boil
Even if your blood is royal
Blessings only come to those who toil

Turning the good earth's treasure chest
As a reprieve from plight
For those who deny being blessed
Also bask in the eternal sunlight

Even though there's a growing need
To understand the crop as much as the seed
For the good earth shall not be turned
Time and again
Without recovering what has been

Encircled or entwined
Are the miracles and secrets Of God's mind
Picking and choosing isn't a mortal game
Nor can the unhealthy find anyone to blame
For those who feel they have some worth
Is a culmination of a contributing birth

Sown and raised on the good earth

Postscript

Bad crops
Can't be blamed on the good ground
Of our earth's deploy
When the purveyor prays not
And grows only to destroy
The only ground we've got

For it's our only security
With the future in its rebirth
We must PRESERVE the Good Earth
Making sure it's here for eternity

Climate will change
Heat and ice will come and go
But plastic bottles in the sea
Is a threat to humanity

Undeniably
We must clean our house
And de louse
Our air our atmosphere

Saving what we hold dear
Our ship to the other sphere

ONE BRICK AT A TIME

Buildings are built one brick a time
The strength is in how well each brick
Is placed in the mortar
And how much effort you can buy for a dime
And how well you spend each quarter

Dams are built one brick at a time
How much they can hold depends
How much water they need to confine
And how well laid the plan decends

Lives are built one brick at a time
Either to be happy or sad
Ironically told by this rhyme
Can come being good or acting bad

We know that mud work and mind
Are like bubbles in a sea do align
Until they make bricks to grind
Then lay each one at a time

I've said it in my design
Making sure my life aft and stern
Is built one brick at a time
Keeping in sight that life is what I earn

For like laying bricks
You must stand back from a reality
And spot the shored up sticks
Through the sticks' and stones' fragility

Then tear apart the existing structures
Till it's a pile of dust
And start rebuilding futures
One brick at a time as you must

Lo luck opportunity and circumstance
Enter into this feat
But also preparation and romance
Are hard combinations to beat

For laying your one brick at a time
One upon each other each day
Our whole existence will rhyme
In the plots and acts we play

Be it music or art
Bach Beethoven and Poe
Lennon Diamond and John Doe
All know that it's the will to start

Even though weak bricks and sticks
Are onerous when they appear
Can be replaced by strong bricks
For bricks of love will be near

With the marriage brick
The family can pick
Building of a caring life
All it takes is the faith brick

And a strong husband and wife

I WENT ON DOWN TO THE CITY

I went on down to the city
To do my work
What a pity
And what I found wasn't very pretty

For there's these people there
Some don't feel and most don't care
Much about a stranger's stare
They've been through it
They've seen it all

Short and fat gay or dike
Lean and tall
To them people are all alike
Just like water running through a fall

Hoards and masses
In the hard-nosed city
It's just the same as time passes
Big man poor man is a pity

Even the lame aren't pretty

I was sent on down to the city
To do my work
What a pity
What I found wasn't very witty
Indifference sitting on a fence
Trying to make a dollar
Out of fifteen cents

And Lord it's no wonder
Society's uptight
Nothing seems wrong and nothing seems right
If you don't hustle you're in for a fight

Fend off the hate and end the spite
With people telling you honesty is trite
Making the daytime turn to night
I went on down to the city out of sight

What I found wasn't a city
As sticks and stones broke my bones
After I didn't pay on my loans
But it really didn't matter
As the fat cats got fatter

I went on down to the pity city
To do my work
What some think is large and very cool
I found stocked with an immoral fool
I came back out of the city
Not having any pity
For what is known as the nitty gritty

What a pity city
Then it dawned on me
How can I blame the city
When the problem is we
The people who ignore the un-pretty

Like any other
Homeless relative or disabled brother
We all need to take the responsibility
For what goes on down there in the city

Because a pretty city is not free
It's certainly dependent upon you and me
To attain respectability
And the feeling of an exciting city

That stands for America the home of the free

FOR IN THINE WILL

For in Thine will
Thy will be done
Like the rising moon
Or the setting sun

Thy will be done

Be you strong or be you weak
Depends much upon what you seek
Is it the trail of the setting sun
Or the heights of the raging gun

Thy will be undone
Now if not soon in life's circle
It may be called a revelation
Or termed a miracle

That the essence of creation
Is to overcome each obstacle
For in effort and revelation
Thy will be undone

And to that impart
The size of the heart
The warmth of a hot toddy
And the strength of the body

For to envision the image
And put it within a mortal's clasp
Depends upon a mental decision
To set the goals you can grasp

Then the sight has been set
And the map drawn
Unto you the rewards beget
Each horizon that buys a new dawn

Burning away the fog
With the rising sun
And the meshing of each cog
Thy will be done

As immortal life has just begun
And the end as elusive as the sign
So in reverence to having fun
A pilgrimage is a way to be thine

Is this preaching a religious message
Or is it a statement of responsibility
For humans to strive for a memory page
Is their own faith and belief in reality

If a former life creates a better life
An after life is thine will be done
You decide you run the ride
I have so far
JR

RUMORS AREN'T TRUTH

I TOLD A STORY TO YOU

You listened to my sooth
And I fooled you good
But my time will come
For the essence of truth

It's like the path of a boomerang
Wings turn inevitably
To bring the rumor back to you
If you throw it with good intentions

The rays of hope and the warmth of love
Relentlessly come back to you
Its destination shall not gather
Dust on the rainbow

But if you throw the boomerang
With distain and ill will
Its track has been set
And its destination will fulfill

The intent with its ascent
Gathering the clouds of a stormy day
Mounting a vicious decent
And for this you must pay

As the rumor comes back to you
On the wings of what you said
Though it may not be true
Your sooth is left for you to undo

So what I say young man
And to this I shall command
That truth is in what your do
Not what you say or understand

For this the boomerang effect
Is relentless for its impact
Though only a simile it will detect
Untruth will fall to its attack

Even though it appears as it comes back to you
That it's a truthful lie
And you don't deal with what you threw
To set the rumor to just imply

You hath forsaken truth for a lie
And your personal sooth will die
For rumors aren't truth
And liars can't fly

BUMBLE BEE

Bumble bee
Oh Bumble bee
How do thee
Fly for us to see
Without wings
Of full capacity
How can thee
Fly so capably

Cripple man
Oh cripple man
How do thee
Climb the highest tree
Without legs
Of full capacity
How can thee
Climb so capably

Grandma White
Oh Grandma D
How do thee
Walk so tall and free
Without a stature
Of full capacity
How can thee
Move so fast and capably

Grandma White
Oh Grandma D
How do thee
See what you see
Without eyes
Of full capacity
How can thee
See so capably

The cripple man
And thee
Must have a
Spirit so great
To walk and climb so tall and free

The bumblebee
And Grandma D
Must have a
Heart so great
To navigate

Smaller than a humming bird
And physically
Your strength is absurd
More than it's supposed to be

Thank God
For the heart and spirit
Of the three
The cripple
Grandma D
And the Bumblebee

Buzzing about my tree

BIRTH OF REALITY

Is disaster that doesn't happen a success

A dream is reality waiting to happen
A fantasy is an illusion unlikely to happen
An illusion is a fantasy until
It's conceived as a persistent dream
In a world bestowing such reality

In a World where
Circumstance rules happenstance
Romance beats out chance
Dreams must advance
To be a real expanse

But hope forgiven that
The moving shadow
Called a dream
With the will to add clarity
By lifting the illusion
Out of fantasy
You suddenly have the birth of reality

Throw in the necessary effort
Without the urge to cavort
Or extort
Pick your vacation destination and resort

You have arrived at the birth of reality
Only to discover it's as fleeting as the fantasy
And as much a conclusion
To an illusion

The Joke is on us
And foolishness is just
If in gest
We trust
In Success or Bust

And then retire our ability to dream
For the lack of steam
And the passion to scheme
Leaving us useless and mean

Wake up and be aware
A dream before
Becomes a nightmare
If you fail to restore

Belief in giving birth to reality

DRY RAIN

Dry my oh my
My skin's so dry
From looking at a
Cloudless sky

Sun is done
Done in sun
To a cloudy day
Opening dirt to clay

During May

Dry my oh my
My palm's so dry
From looking at
A threatening sky

Dust to gust
No friend the wind
Carrying a desert tide
To eyes that cried
As flowers died

Dry my oh my
My thought's so dry
Baked up brain
From a dry rain

Vultures here
Smelling fear
And my last dry tear
For the rest of the deer

Yes a draught is one thing
A desert without hope
Is another
Will our will dry up
Or will Mother Nature spring a cup
That runeth over

With floods of moister
Saving us from disaster
For the Dry Rain to kill
Believing it's God's will
That rain be wet again
As the land is cleansed of sin

THE WIZZARD OF WORDS

The court jester
The traveling vagabond
The preaching preacher
The teaching teacher
Put the words together

Let's sing along
Words of wisdom
Words of a love song
Words of prayer
The masterpiece of the wizard of words

Sketch me a thought maestro
Play me a tune making circles around the moon
Upon your alpha harp
To create a beta illusion
That everything is real

The more words you really feel
For its only afterwards
That you can appreciate
The wizard of words

He's a traveling vagabond
He's a court jester
He's a preaching preacher
He's teaching teacher
Speaking the absurd
Into a meaningful word
For to him it has occurred
That life has blurred
To a wordless mocking bird

He's an artist
Sometimes a departist
And could have been
And should have been
A Magna cartist
Words matter they say
Mind over matter they pray

Do it by action
Or as you play
It matters more what your words display
Form them and
Speak them
Or write a hymn

But no matter what you do
Search for something new
Be it an idea
Be it a question
Be it a voice
Make your choice

Everything in the world has occurred
From the meaning of a word
And you can be self-assured
Of a legend endured
Be you a court jester
Or a traveling vagabond
Or a preaching preacher
Or a teaching teacher
Be the wizard of words

Describing the before now and after words

NICKNAMED

Too many years ago
Like just yesterday
Hidden in memories
To be pushed away
I remember…
The nickname game

My younger sister was sensitive
Prone to fret
With a quick sniffle
And tears so wet

Just for a childish
Kick and hoot
I called her
Rutgers Gabby and
Toot

It didn't make much
Sense to be good
Or covet her
As my sister like I
Should

Little did I know
That later
In passing years
I'd be sorry I didn't
Cater

Cater to a little girl
Soft as hay
Brown hair
Given named to us
Norma Kay

Today she states
She hated those
Nicknames
For the disrespect it creates

Taken away
Was a better
Relationship when
Those nicknames
Came into play
Worse yet
Was an unhappy
Childhood
Creating this little game
Of nickname

That I regret
For this misspent
Trait
Even so I still
Call my kids
And their kids
Nicknames

But with their consent
They were and still are
Meadow
Cricket
Hogan
Sweetie Wheats
"T" Whips
Renegades
Little Leigh
Paree
Three "D's" (devastation destruction and demolition)
"C" Whip

The creature
Sweet Fallon
And Cujo our granddog

All etched into my nickname log

THE SHIELD

Skin is so thin
To withstand
Life's harsh hand

Bruises are so blue
To withstand
Life's hew

Eyes are so sad
To cry
Life's tears

Minds are so confused
To understand
Life's fears

Bruised and confused
Fears and tears
We need a shield to withstand
Life's upper hand

A shield of faith
To form a prayer
With words that care

A shield of love
To form a family
With happiness and clarity

A shield of truth
To form the words
Which protect us afterwards

A shield of thought
To never doubt
What life's about

So pick your shield
Soldiers of faith love
Truth and thought
To defend
Family Charity Honesty
Sincerity

For it's the Children of peace
Who shall be the soldiers
Of Christianity
Of instructive Ideologies
Against extremist warlords
That put down their swords

To shield against
War cruelty fear
And prevent uncommon sense
To end our world's sphere

NEVER CAN WAIT

Now is gone forever
Never to return
Holy is the ghost of now
If we live to discern

Learning from the memory
Of what we were to be
And though we aren't
The holy ghost IS now

Now can still be holy
Return and be redone
With thoughts of everlasting
And an undying sun

Well if we are aware
Fate can change
According to what we care
Holy is the flock we range

Upon a field to rearrange
Since the sheep are no more
Than you are mange
On the neck of evermore

The ghost of now
Will guide you and the Jew
Spiritually and soulfully
In the God we fear is true

Believe in now
And not the end
For Holy the Ghost of How
Is all you need to comprehend

It's your Holy spirit that lives on
Emanating from our mental dawn
Knowing even heaven can wait

For never cannot end fate

LIFE BALL

He formed a game
For humans to play
And society to see
Each day

It has the hopes
And the fears
Of romance
Without tears

Many men and women will
Come and go
With degrees
Of courage to sow

Those very few
With extra soul
Will lead the rest
Up the knoll

For this game
They call life ball
Is played upon
A field open to all

Some will do better
Some will do worse
It's up to each one
To write the verse

And ride the hearse

So play it to the hilt
Don't hold back
For it can't be just felt
Or returned to dust intact

Life ball a winner's game
Striking out is a sinner's fame
Belting the ball for a home run
Is done by those having fun

The fun Life
It's life ball
Before bearing pall
Where there's no last call

SCHOOL DAYS

School days
Car pool delays
Oh where does the time fly
Summer's past don't cry

But good days are to come
As long as we're together for play
Having fun
In spite of school getting in the way

Love and kisses
Hugs and tears
More hits than misses
During these school years

My… my how the years will go by
Graduates will move on
Weddings are in the cue
Then you're on your own

Don't be blue

So as ashes are ashes
And dust is dust
Wipe the moisture from eye lashes
And do what you must

But no matter what you do
Don't miss the buss
You're the driver too
And your school days are the thrust

To being what you must

Love Dad

ELVIS IS DEAD

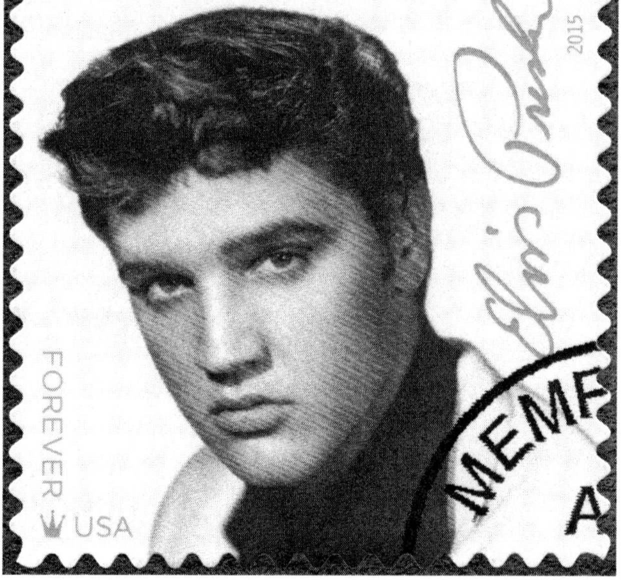

ELVIS IS DEAD

Twinkle… twinkle
Super star
Do you know who you are
Are you an entrant
Or are you far

You struggled for so long
Some things went right
Some things went wrong
A cult born from
The throng

That's your super star song

Make a smile
Take a bow each morn
You've arrived somehow
A star is born

Fame is what it's meant
Platitudes many
Fortunes to be misspent
Shoot the speed and pop the benny

Hold that crowd in your hand
Fly around never land
Until your life is quick sand
And you can no longer stand

You've been high
But now you're down
Can you swim
Or will you drown

It's time to make that sound
To get straight back in round
Get your feet on the ground
Make the changes profound

If you don't
It won't be long
Before they sing
Your funeral song

As the star falls back to the throng
While meeting his calling
To be special being strong
Alas a super star is falling

Into mid air
Someone will catch him
Someone will care
But gone are the worshipper's whim

Soon to be forgotten
He made his bed
Too soon begotten

Elvis is dead

SIDER WEB

Spin your tales
Spin your pattern
Leave the trails
That circle Saturn

It's such a mystery
The way you weave
A strange form of chemistry
To wit the treading fly can't leave

"Stuck upon my universe
Struggling until you die"
To this song and verse
Said the sider to the fly

It's like the web
Of life and death
Stretched out before us
Delicate in its breadth

It's fatal in love and war's crown
On the very Earth in space
A carnivorous trap if you lay down
That holds you in place

In love to the spider lure
The fly vies for its allure
In war the spider lurks
In the minds of the jerks

The tragedy ends
As the spider fends
Upon the fly
And in war the innocent die

The Venus flytrap
The spider's web
Are beautiful to the eye
But fatal to the fly

And you and I

Into its setting
Humans so too are subject to whims
Of the whore or warlord plotting
As the spider lures its victims
Because like the spider
Unless you're the fly
Without the web lure
You'll surely die

Of being love loran
Or war torn
Moral "what you see
Isn't where you will be"

Said the spider to the fly
In the mortal struggle it's you or I

THE OLD BRICK ROAD

The wilderness was tamed
By pioneers whose delay
Was an unsettled land defamed
Making way for a road

For the plow
And a wagon load
The trail was narrow
Only wide enough for a burrow

So they laid the bricks
New and red
Along the crops and sticks
On the fertile bed

The years passed by
Around the clock's hand
To the clicking band
Of horseshoes upon the ply

Until they drove on it
In the iron buggy motor
Bouncing and prancing wit
To the tune of its rotor

Picking up speed
On the old brick board
Back to civilization decreed
We direct our Model T Ford

Much later on a four lane hooter
To Decatur's county seat
The earth is turned to concrete
For taxes and the four seater

For in the moment requires
That the horseless carriage design
Be the sound of slapping tires
Not for growing corn and moonshine

Now in spite of the Interstate
System galore
Our old brick roads are too late
For evermore

The end of those eras and elegance
Are the chance of being born
Into a time when the brick road romance
Falls to the mock of the railroad horn

And the skyway toll booths' scorn

ACE OF EIGHTS

Hallelujah hotshot
You've almost got your straight
All you need to fill it
Is a little ole stinking eight

You've been drawing for those inside
Cards all your life
Can't you understand to gamble with
The man involves strife

You keep going for the impossible card
Trying to stretch yourself and time
Form a foot to a yard
Two feet forward and three back is your crime

Dreaming and scheming that's the beat
Attempting to shape it and plant your feet
In confronting the obstacles with no retreat
Daring you're falling in quest to be great

Finding too late that a joker is really an eight

Hallelujah I'm the Ace of Eights
As poker is pure chance
And drawing the Joker of fates
Makes me a victim of life's romance

Sitting on the sidelines of lotto's trance
Yes life is a gamble and love is a fable
Doing you in or acting to disable
Your desire to run the table

Sevens elevens aces and traits
Gaming for life's Ace of Eights

THE POET

Who is the poet
What does he need
Why should we read or listen
Does he feel something we should heed

The poet's I've touched with my eyes
Seem to be searching out the whys
It's almost artistic as words define
The current that emotions unwind

The poet's I've known with my ears
Use sensitivity confessing their fears
Their feelings are open to all
And unto all they humbly enthrall

The poet that I feel in my fingers
Creates a thought hoping it lingers
If it doesn't he has failed his purpose
Leaving profound words laying on the surface

The poet that I'm striving for in my mind
Has a need for being aligned
To allow him to touch your brain
So you're happier and in much less pain

So poet express your senses for all to see
Reader promise me
You'll try to be much more free
Singer add your melody

It's got nothing to do with wealth
But the poet's inner self
Freeing the thoughts from his heart
To be happy in stillness or concert

It's the music of the mind
And the sounds from the soul

LONELY TRAVELING MAN

From Eureka to Topeka
I have traveled far and been fed

From LA to Monterey
Isn't far but by car

From Missoula to Rantoul
Is by train not by plane

Then from Lauderdale to Martensdale
Just to get away on vacation day

Tuscaloosa is no Honolulu
But in between sights are seen

I'm just a lonely traveling man

From Indianapolis to Annapolis
Be it trailer or new sailor

From Omaha to St. Paul
It's just a skip not much of a trip

From Albuquerque to Schenectady
Airlines take me there so I don't care

Des Moines to Du Quoin
Car hop just one more stop

For the lonely traveling man

That's Macomb to my home
Morton or Chicago scene and in between

Land traveling man rest if you can

Tomorrow is just another day
Car train or plane traveling my way

Never settled to settle down
As I traveled from town to town

With no one else around
On this lonely road home bound

SHADOWS

Following me around a tree
Is this an image of me

Try as they might
To avoid direct sunlight

As black or gray
Shadows dim the day

Tagging along behind
Between the sun and mankind

They're a follower
Of a being's allure

Following the follower
Deciding what to do

Attached to the day time
It takes to get them in line

For sometimes shadows blot
Out the reason for the plot

As themes are now
And bygones somehow

Ever expanding and shrinking
Mimicking what we're thinking

Hidden in the shadows
Until the sun goes

Will they become exposed
And truths then imposed

By the light as is seen
And clarity is the queen

Or as moments lived array
Left for sun lights to betray

Shadows are like love or hate
Can fate be seen before it's too late

Shadows will they ever stay
Or will they decay

With the coming of a cloudy day

INKY AND PEPPY

Dogs and cats
Bygone bats
Doggone gnats
Fetch my fiddle
And I'll play
Hey diddle cats and dogs
In the middle

About life when Kay and I
Were little
And a darn ole black cat
And a tiny Weiner dog
Almost fat
Chasing about
After my paper route

To keep pace
On a four leg race
Back to our hiding place
Inky's black face
And peppy's short
Legged base
Away from others
Different than one another
But like sister and brother

With love we kept her
And him
And he would purr
While peppy with fur
Was now Inky and Pepper

Inky was a night time
Roamer and racer
And Pepper not a loner
But a car chaser

So all was fine until
Inky left one night
As he always did
And never returned
To our Shed

Her cat was gone
Past dawn
And my dog was lame
From chasing cars
As it was her game

Then later Peppy did
As she always did
Chased a car too
Close to the tread
And it came true
Oh my God she's dead

Kay and I were never the same
Her cat was gone and my dog died lame

GET OFF MY DOCK

My ship left me two hours ago
For that port of call
Happiness was the pall
Loving was the port

I'm standing here on this lonely dock
Thinking of that port of call
Joy was the fall
Holding you was the port

What am I gonna do without you
No way to get across that sea
The sea of love that used to be
Before I found I missed the way to you

Funny I didn't know till now
When that boat left on time
That I cared if I ever saw
Your look of love so fine

But now my dock is empty
Moored to destiny
And likely meant to be
Lonely as you're gone from me

Years may come with thoughts of love
And loves may go
But never shall I get over
That love boat I couldn't row

So you're here instead of there
Standing on my dock
Remembering I lost a lover's dare
To a heart too hard to rock

Moor your boat to another
Port and go to hither scenes
Away from my utter
Lonely dock gone to Smithereens

And find your own heart break
Along with regrets to mock
Lost to the bottom of Loser's Lake
Now then get off of my dock

HIM AND HER

A deserted playground sits upon the hill
The sun reflecting upon what it used to be
Gleaming against the slide once a thrill
Sheltered from life by an old folk pin oak tree

A teeter tooter floats astray
With no him and her occupants to work
It's magic of balance and sway
And leverage is gone leaving time berserk

The lasting moments of fun
Are gone to the city
The children no longer run
Physical welfare gone what a pity

Marking time is the rust
Gathering on the swing and chain
Missing is the pump and thrust
Gone are the swinging and candy cane

Lonely is this scene of brown
Void of noise yes past joys
Echoing in the wind with no sound
Gone are the young girls and naughty boys

Forgotten are the days
Him and her just fooling around
Doing stunts and lusty plays
At this deserted playground

When it does occur
Being cool as a square on the merry-go- round
Where everlasting fun was him and her
That life in the past was a play ground

Play no more my melancholy scene
But stand in pride of what you were
Joy to those who hope and dream
Grown up to be healthy adults… him and her

Where that past happiness is never to reoccur
Despite memories found
In a bigger play ground

DEATH OF CAMELOT

A Hard Reign

Many times have passed
Under the bridge
Of what has been
And what will be

Traveled good and
Have traveled bad
Some happy some sad
The masses had a hard reign

If you look back
And remember
That day in late November
When our beginnings

And endings merged
Into a chain that
Never begins nor ends
An anniversary of infidelity

Now remembering what
It was like to be alone
And not wanting to forget
To remember to share

The thrill of being together
But if we forget it's the
Anniversary of the end
A hard reign on our brain

Realization of this
Passing of memories
Into a reservoir of
Appreciation of each other

Dams up the desire
To run away to a
New beginning for the rejected
End must flap in the breeze

Despite loneliness until
It is tethered to a
New beginning a new
November to remember

Damming our sadness on the
Shores of sanity is
Not the purview of the
Selfish one each anniversary

When the hard reign
Occurs each year we
Realize the lasting prize of
The forever chain that goes

About looking for a dock to
Mount for the sake of
Wandering wondering
Finding regretting retreating

And being rejected
Why oh why couldn't satisfaction
Reign in the truth for our sake
As a link in the chain

But November 22 doesn't
Mean the same for all
That came to Dallas… but someday
On a someday morning

The anniversary will rain
Hard on a hard November
Rain will mark the
Time that the factual reservoir

Will fill and spill over
That dam until
It washes away the mystery
Of the who and why

This will be the lasting
Link that pulls the
Beginning and ending
Together into a circle

Of one… no loose ends
Just endless memories
In the heart and soul of
Jack and Jackie

Who now reign in heaven

A nation watching and hoping
When the vision of the shot
Exposed America to coping
With the death of Camelot

They were travelers passing over
The bridge as time passes under
For a 1,000 days he was
To reign

And in five seconds Camelot fell
To a Hard Reign
Anniversary

(RIP the epitaph "here lies the Kennedy's as America lives on"

PAPER ROUTE

Perched upon my steed
I delivered the news
For others to read
About good times and the blues

It wasn't much of a job to like
And I was too young to go to war
So I carried the headlines on a Schwinn bike
About the 89th parallel fear in Korea and more

World War II confronted finality
With the mighty power of the tiny atom
Smashing Hiroshima and Nagasaki
Many said it was Kingdom Come

This is where my views were bred
Would this bring America's proud head
Down for the collateral dead
My heart and pride bled

Peppy and I just didn't know or do much
We sat and folded papers
So others could keep in touch
With the adventure and capers

Of a far off society
With rhythm and blues
Our only reality
On 45 rpm records to choose

Cold and weary too
Or hot and tired
The Register made it through
Until the readers' subscription expired

It seemed my one thought
In those times
Was who had fought
Not these rhymes

Slanted away from the Sunday mass
My customers weren't big people
They're only the simple Iowa class
Informed by that tabloid missile

There was no good news
So the paper boy delivered
To the Protestants the Catholics and Jews
His own views as crowds shivered

And Elvis' dancing legs quivered

The Voice of America played
As the masses prayed

As Radio paid payola
TV came on Motorola

As U-2 fell in a spy flight
Korea was a Communist fight

When our President was an Eisenhower
Music coined as rock and roll power

Then Disappointment... an upset in the Joe Lewis bout
Proved the importance of my paper route

THE ELEVENTH COMMANDMENT NO MORTAL SHALL BEG

No mortal SHALL beg for forgiveness

No mortal SHALL boast with pride

No mortal SHALL kneel with distain

No mortal SHALL stand to pray

No man SHALL kneel to beg

While the boasting mortal is
Begging to stand with pride
He hasn't the poise to wait
For praise for fear
Of distain

If in fact they do

Begging will be their pride

Boasting will be their distain

Kneeling will be their demise

For the sins of begging boasting and kneeling

Won't be absolved by kneeling to pray

Or boasting it away

And Hell will be their absolution

LET BEGGING BE THEIR EPITAPH

Hitler
Stalin
Judas
Manson
Bin laden

All begged for their life and fell on their own knife

OIL ON WATER

Purity
Insecurity
Let my children be

Life is created in the image of
Something that is good
Purified because the newborn mind
Is like the morning of a new day

But like still waters
There will be ripples
As pollution is brought into play
Like oil is to water

Life can contaminate the
Innocent mind
Making it slick and unkind
Like oil on water

The impurities are on the surface
And life becomes a reservoir
Of the mind's oil on its face
With pure water no more

Depriving the mind as a cotter
If and when the oil constitutes
Upon the water
Skim if off before it pollutes

And destroys a healthy mental fate
Skimming involves eliminating
Corrupt beliefs thoughts and trait
From the id and ego that's depleting

The ability to function without flaw
If faith and belief's purifying
Falls short of Shangri-La
That has populated Sing-Sing

While the children of faith
Who believe in making their own reality
Out of facing problems from well-oiled fate
Shall forever be the leaders of the fraternity

The fraternity of oil fighters purifying minds and bodies

SPIDERS AND BEES

To have been
Is the male spider
Finishing the conquest
By dying at the foot of the first courtier

To have been
Is the drone ween
Finishing the nest
By being eaten by the Queen

To have been
Is the human being creature
Finishing a life
By leaving an heir to the future

To have been
Is the female spider
Finishing as conquest assails
By being the Mother of males

To been
Is the Queen bee grace
Finishing the business
By spinning the male's nesting place

To be or not to be the Mother
Is the baby's sanctity
Leaving the nest
By holding the roots of security

To be or not to be the Father
Is the offspring's destiny
Leaving the nest
By spreading the wings of heredity

To be the Child
Is the nest of love and epitome
Building courage to leave
By venturing off their family tree

Making their own honey
Spinning their own webs for money
Planting and growing their own trees
Killing their own spiders and bees

IN A SECOND

How can you love me
For each minute and hour
And hate me in a second
Making us sour

Is it temperament
Personality
Emotions or
Fear of me

Or just gas on your fire
With an accelerator
And an escalator
Without a governor

Like any engine
Yours has pride
Energy Love
Fear or hate
For me

Knowing this changes
My responsibility
To our welfare
Not just your surface
Reactions to me

Cool is better than hot
With a strategic hug
A subtle kiss
A sincere smile

Relieves the situation
And doesn't beg
An answer
Just understanding

Then our partnership
Will not liquidate
Infuriate accelerate
Escalate into a second chance

And has extinguished
The smoke not the fire
Because that fire
Fuels our love

TO FASHION

I spoke to fashion
With my emotion
Took off my clothes
To this new notion

Punk to be in style
With my pierced ear
Long fingernails to file
And no lite beer

Black tight pants
Patted paten leather hair
Shoes on strutted stance
Just so people stare

All to a fashion
Saying little… showing to much
All to perverted fun
Too crass to touch

Look… look Mum
Tell me I'm great
Even though it's dumb
Take a look at my date

Acknowledge I'm your son
With theatrical pride
Just to fashion
The respect to decide

Style and class have died

In a world of
Prada Cassini Chanel Abboud
In the Cloud
Beane Ellis Kardashian Klein Mizrah
Just getting high
DKNY Wang Vuitton Kors Giannini
Shallow and skinny
Gucci Versace
On drugs and itchy

To fashion with class
As a red carpet above the mass
With discriminating fashion
So looking great is fun

MY LIFE KITE

MY LIFE KITE

My kite got hung up in a tree of course
Trying to get free
I almost made it over the forest
But the trees I didn't see

Caught me
In their grasp
Wouldn't let me fly
Couldn't go for the sky

I tugged and tore at
The rein
But couldn't stand
The pain

So in pity I relaxed
Let go stopped pushing
Sat back on my notion
Controlled my emotion

When I no longer could pull
The limbs cushioned my
Wings until they were full
Spread against to fly
Boost off my roost

I made my adieu
With the free wing
Up and away I flew
Only tugged by my string

I was back to bring
Freedom pursuing the last virtue
Of courage with patience
And the first blessing of innocence

The birds have it
Jesus had it
We have it if we don't
Fight for flight

But strive to be a natural high
Doing our own thing
But not alone to fly
With strength to break that string

Held by life's kite tree
And to avoid the next hindrance
If we expect to end the suspense
Takes our desire to be free

Yet fly life above the grasping tree

DISTANCE

Distance between two
Creates resistance between me and you
Happy to hold you if I could reach you
But the distance widens no matter what we do

Like two souls passing time in our own direction
Not by love but by election
To hold you we must comply
Or our love will die

Chasing dreams it just seems
Distance in no way redeems
What we were or what we are
When the distance is too far

So if we want to renew
The fire with desire I must be near you
Come closer shorten the distance
Let me break down your resistance

Otherwise cut me loose
For there's no use
Living with resistance
Widening the distance

It will only result in our
Drifting away the power
Fighting to get closer
To be the music not the composer

Harmony without a melody
For composing beauty
Leaves out the passion
Don't you see love needs a reason

While we make a symphony
The distance between you and me
Without resistance there will be closure
So hold your composure

And come closer

THE SON OF A FATHER

The son of a competent
Raises question of descendant
Into the soul of heritage
For that's the work we wage

As the scales weigh us all
Whether we rise or fall
All we hear is the relentless call
Are we the ceiling or a wall

Sitting in the corner or standing tall

The son of an incompetent
Gives no bearing or virile stunt
Likewise the pride is the brunt
Of the reason for being a runt

For days with the fore bearer
Created an attitude into a stare
Are we dull or much aware
Will we climb or just be there

Above the tracks or laying bare

The incompetent son of a competent
Overshadowed and avoiding the hunt
The competent son of an incompetent
Rising above perception to do the stunt

The incompetent son of an incompetent
What else could be the expectant
The competent son of a competent
Following footsteps could be indifferent

Yet all must eventually walk alone
To the best of their own dismay
The son of the Father to condone
Must find his own competent way

From a father who plants
Doubt and is a son of a sycophant
Never knowing where the apple will lay
Beside the tree or a runaway

Looking for competence his own way

MUTUAL

Tell me your problems
And I'll tell you mine
But do we really care
About each of the pair

Inward feelings of fear
Running down my face
Which we call a tear
Fleeting in any case

Silent signs of attitude
Showing through my language
Coming finally to a sense of gratitude
At any age

Because it could always be worse
As we acknowledge each other and another
Words come out as we converse
First as strangers and then as brother

For no being shall survive
As an island
The need washes us alive
Upon a forgiving land

No being shall love or exist
As a stranger
The companion will always persist
With fate as the arranger

For to hide as you must
Resist as you must allude
You still will accept my trust
If yet our enemies become the mood

Give me your attitude
Give me your
Gratitude
Give me your back

And our fate is mutual against attack

HIGH SCHOOL REUNION

I've been through heart ache
And innumerable fears
But there's no more at stake
Than a high school reunion of 50 years

I thought I would just go
See old friends
And those I know
More for pride than amends

But from the moment we walked in
It became apparent
That those thought friend
Were only going to resent

The way we look the way we live
Yes they were a part of our book
But now it's what we appear not what we give
A browsing wonder is the look

Into the jaws of my own pride
The sum total of it all
Was like a joy ride
About to fall

Shari stopped their clock
But reminded them of nature
Because it seemed to unlock
How they felt about a lovely creature

As for me I've never been free
Of those whom I thought more
Only to discover belatedly
That I'm the richer by not thinking them poor

A reunion isn't a reunion at all
When a fool's a fool
Tending to think small
Even after high school

Fifty year's gone one and all
Never to return me to the bond
Of the purple and gold football
Waving its magic wand

IDLE TALK

You could tell me you believe
But you don't
You ask me to believe
But you don't care

You could betray me
Because you don't believe
Since I believe in me
And I believed in you

Your idle talk no longer interests me
Unless you prove your belief in me
That takes tangible evidence
By your actions

No other proof is acceptable
No other proof is beyond idle talk
Idle talk contains no value
It is cheaper yet to forget

But sincere actions consistent with
Heart felt words purchase
Faith and belief
Above the spinning

Of idle talk
Politicians do it
Parents do it
Opponents do it

Idle chatter
Does it matter
Like getting fatter
Or reading the mad hatter

Does it really matter

It's in the ears of the idle
With their horse bridle
And polo ponies
Being themselves being phonies

Since it's consensual
And the first amendment is constitutional
Don't be judgmental
Maybe it's just mental

So maybe we exercise our right
To not listen or fight
Let them chatter
Because it may matter

While motors idle
The panhandlers dawdle
And rumors prattle
Soothsayers like cattle

Ride bridled on America's saddle

CATCH ME IF YOU CAN

The world tried to catch me
Doing my time
But I put out to sea
To seek what's mine

The storm took me down
Took me under
Round and round with no sound
I paid for my blunder

Only to surface in another place
Playing my same tune
Into outer space
Heard by none other than the moon

Jupiter said hello
Mercury ran away
Pluto stood still and
Mars was here to stay

Flying on earth couldn't catch me
Made me worth only what
A few could see
Till I learned it's my life alone

Like any other stone

Can have its drawbacks
If fundamentally it lacks
In substance and satisfaction
Cause life's need for romance

Can't be served just by chance
And mindless distraction
So let me impart to you
Why we must stay

At a pace with our defined space
Letting the slow disrupt
And the impatient chase
But by no means will everyone catch-up

Leaders lead
Followers follow
Just don't follow the followers
Or try to mislead the leaders

Let all try to catch-up
Before the jealousies erupt
With a failure to understand
That corrupt

Into Catch Me If You Can

AS TIME RAN COLD

As time ran cold
And I became old
No clock could catch me now

I guess sometime untold
Left me uncontrolled
No clock could show me how

The day to pass untold
Just a little bit cold
No clock could pull a plow

This gives reason
To the birth and season
No clock could be a cow

Nor could man be everything
That might ring or sing
No clock could be more than now

The creator created all
The clock the man the stall
No coward could knowingly bow

Undeniably my feet went first
As if time's the RIP hearse
No clock could possibly allow

Without the time to endow
The mother the foal and a worthy soul
Catching time in an hourglass somehow

Giving eternal life with no time
To stop the clock and no end to allow
A cold moon setting on my brow

And as the sun warmed
The devil with a scowl
Made my grave bed... wow

Its freezing now

LIFESTYLES

Talk is free
Love is granted
Time is taken
Hope is assumed

Pride is stilted
Death is sudden
All with no cost to you
But what you decide to do

Lifestyles call collect
And expect fulfillment
As we play at life so we can live
Live to play at freedom

There's no compromise to make it work
Not even work equals this
Perspective unless
We are no longer free

To pursue our dreams
Our pleasures
Illusive treasures
Lifestyles the fruits of democracy

No Bourgeois
No politburo
No Third Reich
No Mafia
No KKK

No inhibition to live
And let live
To try
And let try

Except the golden rule
In a style chosen
Can bluff and free a fool
With inhibitions we thought frozen

Let life warm the highs
Before the opportunity dies
Taking lives without the prize
Read my lips it's the style not the size

WHO SAID LOVE IS FAIR

Who said love is fair
Love's good only if you care
I know I've been there
And love's not fair

Holding out for more
Is the way to ignore
What most lovers store
In the very core of their lore

Tell me you don't need love
And turn around to shove
When you don't get enough
Looking for some better stuff

Till you make it tough

Don't come back with just an apology
When you cut me free
To look for security
Now you want another piece of me

For your futility

The game's we all play
To get our way
And to avoid having to say
Take my love anyway

I'd rather find another
Like sister or brother
Who will not smother
My intentions and discover

Hate's not fair

Believe I now don't care
About your wanting me there
When it's convenient for you to declare
Love's not fair

PAST TENSE

Past tense nonsense
Present line with a rhyme
Most of which is facial mime
For a dollar and a dime

We could all be a prince
If we had the time
Present tense makes sense
Passing time is the crime

With mountains to climb
Fortunes to find
Taken now from hence
Clean hair cream rinse

Get yourself off the fence
Taking the side of chance
For boredom is killing romance
Leaving death to dance

Upon the grave of nerves too tense
Calm can collect
Around what you expect
If initiative isn't wrecked

By too much common sense
Breaking each move into pretense
While what's past
Delays our next cast

For that illusive catch
The biggest bass
Winning the last match
Or missing the last Mass

Yes you didn't get your way

But past tense is worse than "you're passé"

LUFKIN 2526

Interstate 55
The highway parade
Four 18 wheelers are alive
Asphalt has decayed

Through snow to the blessed plain
Plowing the time aside
Sliding by frozen rain
Sorry the map had lied

Sleep tugging at my car
Ripening fruit in my trunk
Dead leaves dissolve afar
While the weather stunk

Wiggling tracks from a falling star
Lufkin 2526 washed and shiny
Passes into my lane then my car
Swerves as my wheels get grimy

Wait a minute
While I climb on your raft
Let me in it
Pulled by a red ball draft

Pull me fore and aft in vane
Into the driving wind
Away from the express lane
Any caravan a friend

While sunshine is a stain
Spreading my shadow
All over the field in vain
The faster I go

As my speedometer checks it
Hear this new sound
A siren a light a cop will get
Lufkin swinging into south bound

No thinking about being killed
Lufkin 2526
Maneuver fulfilled
Peels off the exit

Lufkin 2526 didn't stop
The monster made off with my raft
Tailed by authority's cop
Running off with my draft

Leaving me in its 2526 tracks
While the cop failed to get the facts
Though my eighteen wheeler is in tact
This day can't be in the black

REHIREMENT

Retirement rejected
Put on the side line
Re-hirement injected
For staying in the mine

With intent to torture
Is the age of 65
Telling the future
You're not alive

Relegated to downtime
Put in a permanent mold
Having to redesign
How to avoid the strangle hold

Always productive
And employed
Now we aren't seductive
Nor is our involvement enjoyed

Put on the shelf
For demonstration
Bringing no wealth
To an aging nation

Starting over as a flop
Turns inches into yards
Crawling back to the top
Isn't in the cards

It's full of landmines
Ready to take off the legs
Out from under our confines
Leaving us to what begs

Professionalism is not
Out of the question
If you can show what you've got
Resurrection from gestation

Is it really age that counts
Maybe it's the expense
As the cost of retirement mounts
And experience makes dollars and sense

For each senior's hesitations
Rehirement must deal
With qualifications
And the right feel

Do I want to retire
And don't want responsibility
Or I want to rehire
For my own respectability

We will all have to make
This decision
More than the hoe and rake
When pride is the reason

Any job may be your stake
Then working is just pride
Don't make that mistake
Gratification isn't a free ride

POET or WRITER

A poet is a dreamer
A writer is a story teller
A poet is a redeemer
A writer is a schemer

Can they be both
Or is destiny
Much more frank
By calling the poet a fantasy
And the writer a crank

Of course it depends
On the reader
Who is the equator who defends
The product to be art or a bleeder

This review results
Are more often than not
With many ands and buts
That decides who is cold or hot

And though money is involved
Opinion counts more than currency
While truth is dissolved
By what do you think of me

Myself I want to know
Are my poems by a writer
Or is the writer rhyming flow
Not making something greater

I have written both poems
And novels
Unto each it seems
That verbs are verbs and vowels are vowels

So what's the difference
Is it the sentence
Or the inference
The essence or the romance

In honesty let's not mince
Words are words
And the only difference
Is just common sense

Poems are for honor and the novels for suspense
So I feel I'm a writer of poems
And a poet writing novels
Where the starving artist dwells

Ultimately it's what sells

ALONE TOGETHER

Do you ever feel you are alone
Despite being together
You're on your cell phone
As is your competitor

Society is in the midst
Of the new culture
With a new twist
Of that you can be sure

Whether it's texting
Sexting tweeting
Speaking listening
You are not connecting

With the personal you
It's on long distance
And only a few
Can overcome this resistance

It's a twitter link
With my I-phone
Replacing my need to think
When Siri is in my zone

At no time in my life
Have I been alone
Until I stood up
For something

I stood up to walk
To Run
To graduate
To wait as a birther
To fight

But all with someone
Interacting not faxing
Or hacking
Or texting me
Right next to me

Texting together
Is like sun during stormy weather
Trying to ignore
The person right next door

COWARD

Who is a coward
With a word
"A person who runs away
And all we see is the back of their salute"
Even disserting their bed

Who is a soldier
With a word
"A person who runs ahead
And all we see is the back of their head"
Protecting the Fed

Who is a loser
With a word
"A person who runs away
And all we see is the back of their hand"
Over playing their risk

Who is a winner
With a word
"A person who runs ahead
And all we see is the back of their fist"

Who is a leader
With a word
"A person who runs for office
And all we see is the back of their salute

Who is a follower
With a word
"A person who runs for votes
And all we see is the back of their boot"

Cowards aren't soldiers
They aren't winners
They aren't leaders
But they're all three when cornered

Courage comes by no choice
By no voice
By no option
So cowardice is an adaption

Of fear converted to courageous action

BOTTOMS UP

I took the plunge
Into the unknown
With nothing but a nudge
And my goals were overthrown

Tendered a challenge or two
Nothing smooth
Just you can construe
Somewhat a grove

And a lot at the helm
Bottoms up awash then
Overwhelm
Turned upon my back to them

Fore and aft under attack
Pride and ego hurt
Nothing to do
Can't avert

Perceived fright and doom
Turned night into hell
And the past into gloom
While reality rung my bell

Drinkers have remorse
The promiscuous get a divorce
But the bankrupt
Feel the bottom come up

While the head
Goes down
Spinning values
Round and round

Until they can be stopped
Slowing then starting
Into another for estopped
Another venture

With a gun shy look
At human nature
Strung out but coming round
My bottom hasn't lost anything it hasn't found...
Bottom's up... It's a new round

DIGNITY

Feeling good about your values

No life can live in confinement
Without perversion of values
The lack of freedoms… speech
Thought consent reaction
Tears down the resistance to evil

Any life can live up to
Expectations set too low
But living down high
Expectations lowers
One's confidence

Who can quite know which
Road to take
Those who take one live on
With high acceptance for effort

Those who hesitate lose their
Dignity to doubting their values
Sacrificing progress to stagnation
Until it becomes a bad habit

A survivor is just that
A lowering of values until
All is lost to winning
Back dignity

Once retrieved
Dreams can be conceived
Actions taken are believed
And dignity once again is achieved

Give me dignity or give me death
To my last dignified breath

GOLD DIGGER

GOLD DIGGER

Gold can be found
In a heart thought cold
But a mind of gold
Is never old

Taken into the shale
Or stone
Turned to pale
When all alone

The dying time is yet to come
For most are dead
And there's some
Only to a wake misled

But my love is never old
Pushing away my fear
And my wake is gold
As tomorrow is my career

Asleep at the control
The masses call out for help
Afraid to touch a soul
Or express itself

Headless helpless loveless
The wake of time
Is the death of a caress
And nothing is ever mine

Except there is the creature man
Seeking a mate to understand
Simple as bird in flight
Turning bloody red to white

A gold digger is in sight
Disregarding the plight
Wasting by day
Contaminating by night

Foliage dies in a winter storm
Yet it lives beneath the hearth
When spring turns us warm
By future burning days on earth

I can wait
For the wake of mine
Thinking our love isn't too late
Making all ages fine

And though the King is dead
While the Queen is gone
The Prince of youth is wed
Upon the greening lawn

Ah spring is now my heart
Pushing the roses through my mind
Pulling together those now apart
And your wake is only mine

A mine of gold found
While heaven bound
Formed as a body of thine
Thought a jewel alone

A wake can mean
The gravity pulling us along
Until our death has been
So we will awake to belong

Together once again

DRIVEN

His obsession was driving him crazy
His obsession is now driving him forward
Now is the difference
Now the obsession is fundamental

A catalyst to the confession
Once used as the device
Effort in cessation
Was strictly incidental dice

Fundamentals of finding the path
Consist of incidentals plus the other half
The other half of a whole craft
Practice practical practice
Makes for perfect fundamentals

Thinking
Doing
Rethinking
Redoing

The absolute obsession drives
Me toward
The skill and the will
To be driven forward

Practicing that
The greater good
For the lesser evil
Is not happiness
But an endless chase

While the greater good
Against the lessening evil
Is a reason to be driven
Forward with obsession

SONGWRITER BLUES

Songwriter blues that bring the news
Eat your peanuts
And drink the booze
We've all been listening to
Songwriter blues

Time's ticking away the time of day
With me crying in my beer
Because you aren't here
It's all bad news
From the songwriter's blues

Words coming in ones and twos
Girls and boys are here to choose
Hassled by the songwriter's blues
The guitar picker up on that stage
Making it nightly but not for the wage

Soothing these cowboys
Just for the night
Are all the rage
Most of them look like they've
Stepped out of a cage

Looking me up and down
Like a new guy in town
The bartender he don't care
He's just gonna serve me another beer
With the same old sneer

That'll be a buck buddy
Strange scene it's to study
With time passing by
The air all muddy
With no hope and feeling cruddy

Thinking about you
How we used to be two by twos
Not this reflection of the
Songwriter's blues

Hey bartender give me some more booze
I've paid my dues

HALF OF THEM

Don't know I'm here or there
They'll come back and I will be gone

I don't care about moving
It seems alright now
But moving on a holiday
Just isn't right somehow

My friends and those I know
Who saw me for the last time
Will wonder where did I go
Leaving on a holiday seems a crime

Sure wish it could have been summer
And we all knew in advance
About our going really I'm feeling dumber
Without this longer chance
To say goodbye
To give the reason why
To explain and not cry

Cause half of them won't know I'm gone
And the other half will never phone
But "so long" my new friends
Are my new chance to belong

My children don't feel the way I do
They would rather stay
But we have choices very few
Necessity has the last say

Pack the bags and get in the car
Don't look back
They won't care how far
We are going to cut the slack

Our fortunes are to be made
Elsewhere so don't despair
This move will allow us
To live in a house not a bus

The schools are the best
Our home is as good
And better than the rest
In a fabulous neighborhood

And we will be in a bigger trust
Opportunity for all of us
Our future so bright
You will have to wear shades at night

So wait and see this is no time for fright

LIFE SUSTAINING

Life is sacred
Death is less terrifying
Prolonged life is moral
Prolonging death is immoral

Life has ultimate value
Death transcends the other values
Does this answer the question
How long do we sustain life

Is it a personal decision
Or a family reason
A physician incision
A government mission
Or a judge's admission

Circumstances hold us all
In its hands
Reality dictates the decision
If we relent to it's commands

Life is a bubble
And we sit precariously on it
Thinking we make less trouble
So we don't fear it

Life is sacred
Death is less terrifying
Prolonged life is moral
Prolonging death is immoral

Are we going to prolong life
Or are we prolonging death
Seems like an easy choice
But as we have found out

This is the hardest question to answer
Depending on who will give the response
The patient should take priority
But is the patient competent or ensconce

If not then who is competent
To give the final decision
The physician is most qualified
But the least likely to convince

Will the family the spouse the authorities decide
It comes down to "do we want the Judge to decide"
If not then who

Life is sacred
Death is less terrifying
Prolonged life is moral
Prolonging death is immoral

Obviously it is a judgment call
And the Judge will make
It if we don't
Prolonging death is immoral
As death is likely transcendent

Therefore odds are

We are deciding to let God make the choice
Don't prolong misery for prolonging life
For death is an intervention not an ending
Prolong the next life not this one

SING YOUR OWN SONG

I hear you singing in the shower
I hear you talking in your sleep
I find you thinking out loud
I see you saying what you believe
I find you dreaming in silence

You ask me for approval
With your eyes
You listen to my silence
With your heart

With these emotions we live together
With each other we live with emotions
By singing our own song
We can express our own space

We have come together in love
We have struggled together in haste
We seem to let others influence above
Our own ears and good taste

Shut out the static
Listen for the clear message
Just ask me for approval
With your eyes
Then listen to my silence
With your heart

What do you hear
Is it a love song
Or is it just not clear
Why we will always belong

To our own drama
Sung and played together
With an orchestra
Of our peers… eyes and ears

I hear you singing in the shower
I hear you talking in your sleep
I find you thinking out loud
I feel you saying what you believe
I find you dreaming in silence

Our body language is more than defiance
It's our own song's vision of romance

EMOTIONS

I got a handle on my shovel
I got a job to earn my pay
But my emotions are in upheaval
And keep getting in the way

It seems life is spent chasing
Chasing a job during the day
Then at night we are romancing
So we can share where we lay

Two sided lifestyles in our time
Causing us problems as they betray
The results of getting out of line
If we let our morals decay

God and offspring are the spectators
Letting us feel emotions as we play
Much like the tireless gladiators
They then let obsession get carried away

Dying from a debtor's lifestyle
Dishonor every day
Never knowing all the while
The price we'll have to pay

To test our emotions
To test us of our will to say
Leave me to my devotions
Which are to love and then play

For it's our work which must root us
Not pleasure nor in its search should we dismay
To such we must carry shallow lust
And let love rise from our emotional disarray

Stability is the lasting reward
Devotion to emotion is not
Promiscuity will take us downward
Wasting all the good times forgot

Having the good wife
And having a good job yes
But the essence of happiness
Is having a good faithful life

Hopefully with our first wife

SAYINGS

Be what you want to do
Don't do what you want to be

Facets of the past create
Trials of the future
So do your days with
Thoughts of the days you borrow
From your past

Be yourself do your best
Calm the urge to build the nest
Then foregoing rest
You fail the greatest test… your happiness

What do you want most
Is it love
Is it wealth
Is it fame
Or are all wants the same…
Decide as it's your game and blame

A figment of perceived joy
Standing before the discriminating world
As blind as a decoy
Waiting for the prey as we pray

What good are our words
Do they precede us or are they
Merely a statement for afterwards
Not knowing is denying destiny

Live today as if it is gone
And tomorrow is not a new dawn
With the night everlasting
And daylight welcomes your not wasting

Be what you want to do
Don't do what you want to be

For the sake OF YOUR LAST AT BAT

THE POET IN ME

Is it my place to state your
Philosophy
Opinion
Problems
Issues
Beliefs
Life's goals
Love affairs
Habits
Aspirations
Religion
Politics
Future
Past

My answer is hell no
My role is to get you to think about your own
Philosophy
Opinion
Problems
Issues
Beliefs
Life's goals
Love affairs
Habits
Aspirations
Religion
Politics
Future
Past

And use it for your future thoughts about
Philosophy
Opinion
Problems
Issues
Beliefs

Life's goals
Love affairs
Habits
Aspirations
Religion
Politics
Future
Past
Then be your own poet like me

THE MAKER AND THE UNDERTAKER IN US ALL

God made Adam
Who laid his rib to bare
For the life of Eve
As we're all waiting there

Yes the Maker of us all
Could only start the process
Standing up the Neanderthal
To beating on his chest

From that point forward
We were on our own
The land the days were hard
Until a mate saved us from being alone

And even then until the offspring
No full meaning occurred
Nor did we learn to sing
Much more than a primitive word

But the siblings followed love making
To test our patience
Sharing each undertaking
Giving the future substance

The satisfaction cut through
Our fears and frustration
Giving hope for the new
And sprouted strange feelings of elation

While THE MAKER kept watch
But interceded little
Leaving us to catch
The prey and fill the kettle

Then was much the same
As it is forever
Survival is part of the game
We must always endeavor

And then when we have a warm den
Leaving us time to think
We can conceive of the desires to win and sin
Bringing us to the brink

Ah yes it was the Maker
Who gave us our chance
But it's the undertaker
Who we must always romance

And keep at bay
In ourselves
Until judgement day
When the Maker tolls the final bells

PUMPING GAS

I smell lava soap
Too sweet to be clean
Too heavy to be soft
Too overpowering

Hands are hands
So why exchange the natural
For the disinfected
I smell cheap soap

Pumping my own gas
Is an understandable nuisance
To be sure but not lasting
In its odor
Like the cheap soap trick

Which is worse tells it all
You've washed away nature while
Touching is relegated
To un-touching affairs

Like
Medicinal drinking
Odorous hands
Stinking armpits
And smelly rubber bands

Hands shouldn't reek of a
False palate
It makes my bridgework
And Silicone chest
Turn to putty

Only a dope would like lava soap

BUILD HOPE

Hope is built on tribulation
Not just speculation
It takes faith to get it
The feelings want it and urges bet on it

For doubts wander
From thought to thought
While hope is built on work
Not wished or bought

With effort
One must exert time not fear it
Upon a persistent determined clock
While longings dispel the spirit

It takes time to build hope

The postulate of needless
Wonderings of
"Will hope built on the
Momentous blunders
Of history be just one hope away
From senility"

No... history says hope is built on trial
And error
Which criticism will always beguile
Human frailties to stop in terror

Relegating themselves to single file
Following the followers
Into the River Nile
Not to be baptized as hopeful scholars

But left behind to lotto's chance for dollars

A HEART OF GOLD

Every body needs a heart of gold
And when you don't mine it
The body dies

Every sunset needs a body
And when it rains
The heart pains

Every lover needs a reason
And when it isn't there
The body doesn't care

Everybody needs a lover
And when you turn it out
The mind fills with doubt

Everybody needs a loving body
And the time is now
No time for wondering how

So come to me everybody
In the universe
And I'll tell you in my verse
About needing somebody

To have and hold
Is life's only fool's gold

A vein in every heart
Awaiting to be mined
For everybody to find
Even by the selfish and blind

Like the gold diggers of the past
When true love didn't last
Panning the heart for gold
Pulls true lovers apart

But the real gold isn't
For everybody
For not everybody
Has the heart made bloody

By gold diggers and tire kickers
Who are only looking for quickers
The other side of the quickee
Wanting sex only for ME

By rejection then affection
When true love is built
On reflection
Not deception and guilt

So give me a true lover
Who is looking for more then bed
Not just under the cover
And I will give you thee wed

A love that's golden through and through
Ready to be mined by you

HABITS TOO HIGH OR LOW

How high is low
Are you bought or caught
In a habit you hadn't sought

How low is high
In the flight to buy
Happiness you couldn't try

How can we go
Low or high as a habit
Before we know we're getting high

Tonight we may find
Tethered we are high
Separate we unwind to a failing sky

No way to quell a bad habit
You or I
How low is low until we defy

Can't just cry wolf
With life bearing down on us
How low is high losing ground with habits we buy

Memories we once found
Dissolving into yesterday
Fleeting like a sound they fade to another buy

How high is low
As a sense of desperation
When distilled elation goes awry

Low is a street drug to sell or buy
No kindness in such love
Creates a hell I'm thinking of… the habit

Shall never quell our fear
And doubt of ourselves being
Worthy of the habit of love

If the habit is too high or low
Keep it simple just quit… please try
To kick yourself and the bad habit will die

Before you do

HURRY

Hurry the seventh mortal sin
A loser's game of chance
And obsession to win

Hurry is the mother of worry
No simplicity just travesty
No time for love or happiness

Rushing here then there
A mental hell with time wasted
Personal losses with feelings untrusted

Futile work and spoils
No lover settles for a mistress
As futility is a just casualty

Of time's obsession and confession
Before this dome of futility rests hurry
Where Satan dwells

Hurry is the obsession of scurry
No stability just intensity
No time for true romance

Rushing here then there
No heaven just time wasted
No one wins with goals left busted

This confession calls out to you
As an obsession that we must carry
If we thus worry

But worry is due to hurry
When worry and scurry
Are missing the right turns of life

Unto which we must hurry
Before we bury
Ourselves in worry

THE SAME DIFFERENCE

All our lives we dream of being different
We strive for independence and our freedom
Some of us achieve a sense of self-expression
We become a spring in off season

But the truly different ones are the same
That look in their eye
The gait of their walk
The smile and the way they get low to high

Most of all it's more than chemical talk
It's a style the top of the rock
That layer of silk
The leader of the flock

Look into the essence and scene
And you'll find the same difference
It's in the SEAL at sea
It's in the descendent of the Marine

It's in the heart of Tis of Thee
It's in the heritage of the Queen
It's in the limbs of our tree
It's in Kip Kim Kelli and Christie

And today I'm convinced
My wife and I are the fence
Separating the same infants
A credit to the same difference

To this I give credit to where
It belongs
Coming to us from our heirs
Speaking to us in their poems and songs

That Kip sings
Kim draws
Kelli conceives
Christie achieves

The same difference is in our
Grand children
Great Grand Sons
Inherited from

Our Fathers and Mothers and the Holy one

LOOK ALIKE

Look in a mirror
Check out the reflection
It's very clear
We're not just alike

But that's a deception

We've conceived offspring
Influenced their lives
Tried to give them everything
Even when it seemed contrived

And without a form or pattern
The limbs grew intact
Libra Scorpio Sagittarian Cancer
To the signs of Zodiac

Until it became me in you… you in me
We go our separate ways
Into different days
But the pull of later days

Attracts us to be just alike

We're wedded by minds and psyche
Because our heredity is always true
We begin to think and live alike
As different facial bodies grew

For we chart our own course
In our own way
Avoiding remorse
We are still one each day

Mirror mirror now I see
How you are me and I am you
As each one is greater
Than the sum of two

LOVE HAS NO LIMIT

Love has no limit
If you're in it
Hate has no summit
If you wage it

Life has no limit
If you defend it
Death has no limit
If you don't end it

Work has no limit
If you extend it
Vacation has no limit
If you amend it

Marriage has no limit
If you mend it
Divorce has no limit
If you defend it

God has no limit
If you intend it
Satan has no limit
If you trend it

Children have no limit
If they attend it
Parents have no limit
If children offend it

Friends have no limits
If you send it
Enemies have no limits
If you rescind it

Lovers have no limits
If they end it
Haters have no limits
If they bend it

Writers have limits
If they vend the similes
Readers have their limits
If the writer's wind is faint

Poets have no limits just endings

INFINITY

FINITUDE *the state of having limits or bounds*

Do we live in a finitude
Do we limit our life to infinity
Are we treating everything as a finality
Is today the last day of our life

If not why do we worry about yesterday
Why do we worry about tomorrow
Why do we worry at all
Worries are not spring, winter or fall

They don't happen on a schedule
Unless you're concocting them
Making them happen by honoring them
Giving them reality

Rather than turning hope into positive acts
We dwell on something that doesn't even exist
Most times the anticipated never happens
Or it is only half as bad as we were envisioning it

Happiness isn't not being unhappy
Why create unhappiness by worrying about what if's
Because what if's depends on our actions
We can control that if worry doesn't get us to doubt

Then do the unmentionable… is not to act
In a happy and healthy manner
It's common sense yes
It's logical yes

Is it our habit pattern… hell no
We have been brain washed by our parents or past
And our present vision of what if
Even when it's twisted by fear

Why do I write this as a poem or prose
Because I'm working on convincing
Myself that I'm doing something positive
I suppose

And infinity isn't the reality we reach
It's practicing what we preach

FAIREST OF THEM ALL

FAIREST OF THEM ALL

Kimber Leigh
Your mother and I have watched you grow
From that sweet little girl we love so
You and Christie were quite a pair

I can remember the crowds
Used to stop and stare

For you were more than cute
You had sunshine smiles and giggles to boot
Your mom and I loved to take you with us
Because of all the fuss… you brought to us

Of course you've got to grow
You've got to mold
You've got to know
That there's a future out there to have and hold

And that's the reason you grew
A body a mind and a talent equaled by few
And most certainly we had our times good and bad
But I can't really recall
Any which were overwhelmingly sad

We did things as family cahoots
In giving you our wings of a feather
Establishing the roots
We're held together

So you could fly from the nest
So you could flock with the rest
And determine where you would fit best
For life tends to be a test

And such we are so proud
That we have been allowed
To be the parents of Kimber Rhoads
Who will carry heavier loads

In expressing her feelings
In establishing her heights
Without human ceilings
Nor floor for stairs and flights

Being an expression
Of her Mother and father's creation
To raise a child of the world
With her beauty unfurled

Though flying away may be hard
And our emotions somewhat jarred
This is what we've been preparing you for
And as you know there is always an open door

For the children who are lovingly bred
Shall return to visit their first bed
To rekindle the memories
And look at the pictures

And play old games and tunes
Which are a reflection
Of the happy summer afternoons
And the chattel shall always be there
For you know your Mother and I will always care

To hold you when you need us
To help you get up when you may be down
And to this we have done our part
We have put the love for life in your heart

And when the epitaph is written
About what your siblings think of you
They will have to use gold lettering
Flacked by a Picasso blue

Though you must now totally understand
As you have your own children
Who are trying their wings to leave and land
As does the birds of a feather doves and wren

So wish them all the good graces and luck
Which are brought by preparation and effort
For things you did not duck
Their outcome is more important than their retort

For you are
Of a fiber and fabric
We've wanted for you
Since you were two

Loving talented loyal
That was woven by the heritage of your ancestors
And the pride of your brother and sisters
Into the cloth we now are proud to call

Kimber Leigh Lawrence the fairest of them all

Very truly yours Dad

THE IVORY TOWER

The Ivory tower
The essence of power
Not a place for the dower
Nor those that cower

Says those who are there
Intellectuals spirituals mortals
Are their opinions fair
Are they closure or portals

To be in charge of circumstance
Because of their theories and stance
For knowledge is the parlance
Of those who get the chance

Our society puts much importance
Pomp prance and happenstance
Leaving the results to romance
Watering down the power of the advance

For it's the mortals' fix
That must take the theories
Principles equations metrics
To implement no more than analogies

Realism criticism and any ism
Is a start not a conclusion
For enters opinion and reason
To deal with the changing season

Prognosticators evangelists and visionaries
Live in their own Ivory Tower
Viewing the world and missionaries
As their source of funds and power

Politicians professors bureaucrats pundits
Lording over their flocks
Holding onto the backs of the fat cats
Bearing down to tax their stocks

Capitalists realists and Presidents
Are in charge of the herd
Taking on the theories and precedents
Professed by the Ivory Tower's word

Be it the Constitution or the Bible
We must live by law and rule
For to that we are dedicated to be stable
Until we run out of fuel

For the Enterprise we know as earth
Must honor the sanctity of the individual
That ensures all have worth
While the planet is kept cool

So it's the Popes the Leaders
Of the world of affairs
Keeping the ivory tower breeders
Down to the Great Earth's cares

That being life liberty and peace
Of Governments for the people
By the people
Of the people

Keeping the Ivory Towers thinking
And the real world working together
For peace and prosperity making
The profitable missions of our maker

For we all are makers of our own undertaking
Despite the leaning Ivory Tower of Power

ARE YOU LISTENING

I never used to listen to the wind blow
I never used to watch
Your eyes darting to and fro
I didn't notice your hands when you talked

Nor how you place your feet
When you walked
Or your legs crossed
When our conversation balked

All I listened for were words
Merely sounds like the chirping of the birds
So I found I didn't know you
I thought I loved you
But there was something that wasn't coming through

I was missing your depth
That you kept hidden
Beneath and between the lines
And lurking in the confines
Of what you were forbidden

Namely your gentle ways
But during one of our bitter days
When I thought I'd really earned your praise
You turned away so I would have to listen
To what you didn't say

Or get out of your way
I watched your back to see how you were going to react
When the dawn became the fact
The light spread across my face
Causing a twinkling in my eye

That said more to me
Than your lusty cry
I knew then I'd been missing you
Not hearing silence or feeling your sigh
Not knowing what was true

For your body was speaking
A language that was unspoken
More than just a passing verbal token
It was physically demonstrated
When our relationship was abated

In the aura you created
For as you moved and looked at me
I could now clearly see
Your whole being was committed to me
"But only if you listen to me"

And to her everlasting credit… I did

Reading this and understanding why
Are you looking your spouse in the eye
Listening and giving her your ear and sigh
Or are you just a passerby

Saying "I wonder why she won't look me in the eye"

TOMORROW A MAN

A man is an inhibited boy
A boy is carefree
He thinks of life as
A play toy

He smiles
When he wants to
He cries when he
Feels like it

And you never know
What he'll do
He mimics his parents
If they want him to

He only rebels
At being different
And never wants
To be called lazy

He's only content
When he's a little crazy
And his passing to manhood
Is sometimes sad

If he's the only boy
You've ever had
With a girl
Being the focus of being glad

Then as a man
He becomes more careful
He thinks of life as
Some time to fill

He only smiles when he
Has to
He cries in private
And tells his children

They'll have to wait
Until he's through being
The man failing to understand
What makes a man

Tomorrow isn't what they
Want to hear
When today
Is what they fear

Grow up Dad
It's your job
To turn something bad
Into a reason to be glad

Because boys will be boys
And toys aren't your kids
Positive attitudes makes or destroys
Their lives and adlibs

Into their own kids

Then he's much more intense
And all things
Must make sense
He mimics society

If he's following the leader
Or he defies sobriety
If he's the leader
Looking for followers

He's the same boy
But a different person
Some call it masculinity
I call it a pity

That the boy in me
Isn't the same as the man in me
So I could tell my son
How to stay the same

Even though tomorrow
He must be a child's man
In grownup clothing
With a guiding hand

EMOTIONS

The emotions of life
Are motions from pride
A predictable tide
Of highs and lows inside

That create feelings
Feelings for one self's fate
Feelings for others as
Contentment or resentment

In love or hate

Feelings from positions
That we act out
Reflecting our emotions
Though the actors are in doubt

Not feeling the same plea
Not speaking the same words
Being different in degree
Like the flight of the birds

That's confined predictably
To motion within a particle of snow
With a fixed anatomy of time
As the tides come and go

Waiting to flow in a current
Until it explodes from inside
Reflecting contentment or resentment
And exhaling love or hate or pride

Emotions are the same as the rip tides
They rise and fall
But must eventually subside
To be taken seriously at all

May require a honey moon at Niagara Falls

AS TIME PASSES

The passing of time
The quiet notes of yesterday
The subtle rays of tomorrow
Oh it's a fine passing

Aging each frailty
Improving each strength
Until the sands of today are gone
And yesterday is forgotten

As we are plunged into the future
The passing of a second
So small we hardly notice unless we listen
To what it beckons

The passing of a minute
No matter how minute
Without its breadth to eternity
The passerby won't believe its root

The passing of an hour
Is a sad event if it's our
Last breath and the life of a flower
Is cut short without a rain shower

The passing of a day
What a final also ran
To the entombment by the undertaker
And the epitaph of a passing man

Reliving the lost moments
Quoted in the messages of last rites
So final is the falling annual calendar
To restore those fleeting days and nights

Or the resurrection of a lifetime
Neither within reach or the tether
As just living the last second
Of every minute sixty times better

As those days are eternally gone
From the sundial
That ceases turning days of gold
And you have more time for getting old

A deception as time passes infinity
Into a continuum of an endless journey
Time isn't a sun dial or hour glass
It's eternal energy as you pass

Flowing along the passage of time's compass
Into the crystal ball of carnation

WORST HAIRCUT

Hair styles were battles
In the fifties and sixties
As Elvis and the Beatles
Exposed their pixies

My flattop
Certainly didn't set sail
To the Beatles mop
Or Elvis' duck tail

My dad saw to that
And unless my head
Was flat
He'd not pay the bread

And my barber
Was in his pocket
With his hands he'd harbor
The style on the docket

It was my worst haircut
When I wanted it to grow
He wouldn't give me but
Of a duck I wanted so

Not until I finally rebelled
My hair was so flat
I was compelled
To resort to butch wax

And a baseball hat
To hide my feeling
Of this and that
Ducking tailing stealing

My attraction to girls
Until in eighth grade
I let it grow curls
Training the duck made

Style into an Elvis tail
Blue suede shoes without fail
The trail for the tenth grade
Chick parade

Never again to get
A buzz cut
My dad was in debt
To a duck's butt

Because the hair affair
Gave me the confidence
To take the dare
And get romance

FRIENDS OF A FEATHER

Flocks and herds
Cows and birds
Coveys and packs
Dogs and cats
Feet and inches
Batches and bushels
Pecks and dozens
Aunts and cousins

Mothers and fathers
All together
All in common
Forming their community
Embraces here
Loving there
Strength is summoned
In their unity
Friendship is much the same
Not for attention
But a loving game
Played by the strong
To help the lame
Backed by the will
To heal the sick
And cut to the quick

While the slow clean up
After the quick
When the strong
Rights the wrong
It isn't the rich
That helps the poor
It's the friend next door

Goose and gander
Rooster hen
Friends of a feather
And next to kin
Horses and cattle
Fish and fowl
Soldiers are for battle
Friends are lovers
Or the closest pal

That's the story
That's the dream
Tell me who you seem
On your friendship team
Oh friends of a feather
Flock together
Huddling from stormy weather

The weather of life
The days of strife
Be it stormy
Be it bright
Be a friend
To protect the weak we defend

Feast or famine
Rich or poor
Only family
Shall mean more
Than friends of a feather
In stormy weather
Providing hope

In the middle of night
A friend defies fright
Defuses plight
Embraces flight
The higher the kite
Providing arms for the fight

With the hope to endeavor
Friends are forever

COTTON CANDY HEAVEN

Cotton candy looks so great
Pink and red
Just good bait
When I see it
I just can't wait

Till I get my first bite
And my hopes deflate
It's because cotton candy
Looks like Champaign
But tastes like Brandy
All sparkling and lame

Like my girl Mandy
Till you bite in
And find your mouth all sandy
This is the way of most people's last day
They wait for Heaven and don't even pray
Right up to Judgment Day

But when the time comes
And you've spent your life on crumbs
Heralding God to the deaf and dumbs
Only to find cotton candy
Can be bought at Lums

Heaven cotton candy heaven
I've heard about you since I was seven
Believed in you since I was eleven
Even knowing God was not David Niven
Just looking at you got me craven

Now that I'm ready to take a bite
Looking upon that alluring sight
I begin to feel the fright
Of what's behind tasting so light
But that sugar will destroy my diet fight

Cotton candy can be no more
Flashing out the classy amour
Chilling me to the very core
Inspiring me to go to the ice cream store
Or make a snack from an apple core

Don't take me I'm young yet
I've got so many things that I regret
I've never ever taken the time to set
And contemplate what I would get
From that sticky stick of cotton trick

My vision of cotton candy heaven
That I saw at seven
And believed in at eleven
Says goodbye like David Niven
For what I've not been cravin'

I thought it something which it's not
Just like the substance of an ink spot
With lessons yet to be taught
No way of knowing it would happen
To Cotton Candy heaven

All sticky a sickly pink and red
Over takes my hands and face
Requiring a bath before bed
Not being what I should chose
For the weight I've got to lose

Now I find myself
With a shot and beer
My red wine near
Finding I feel just dandy
Without Cotton Candy

If I can have a shot of brandy

IF THE CLOCK DOESN'T TICK

If the clock doesn't tick
Is the time of day wasting away
If the chimes don't ring
Is it too late to hum and sing

If the words don't mean anything
Is there love and a reason to give a ring
Is there truth if the mouth doesn't lie
And you can't believe in youth

If the clock doesn't tick
And the chimes don't ring
And love isn't everything
Truth is taken from the youth

And all that's left is uncouth
For time is turning on our sweet tooth
In the head of bangers
Has-beeners and out for me angers

But let's not be disillusioned
For such an event to be our curse
When time's still a misspent conclusion
And we marry for better or worse

To keep the clock ticking
The chimes ringing
For the love making
We will be blooming the truth

In our confession booth

LOVER'S HIGH

I get high on love
When I think of you
It's not often
But it's something I do

It's a natural high
Takes me higher than the sky
More than any drug you can buy
Not wanting to ever say goodbye

Even the first love won't die
For being held in loving arms
With that memorable kiss won't lie
An eternal feeling of your charms

When I'm alone and feeling blue
It's not a yearning
That gets me high on you
Its love burning

I know it has to be
For loving you is a part of me
As eyes are meeting
Feelings are made to see

And ears to hear the harmony
I'm high on love
Way down inside of me
Feeling the force of matrimony

For in love the soul can thrive
Keeps your memory so much alive
Memories of what used to be
Memories of why feeling eyes can see

The visions once thought a fantasy
I'm at the height of epitome
I'm high on love
It's got hold of me

If and when it all ends
Making peace and amends
Partings as best friends
Something love always defends

That lover's never part
The hurt never mends
Until the hole in my heart
Heals when another high begins

I'D BE NOTHING

If you didn't love me
I'd be nothing without you
Buried as a man
In a lover's quicksand

You'd be better off I know
With someone you can talk to
And not this crazy impatient man
But take my love and try to understand

That I'd be nothing without you

I couldn't face each day
Read or write or make my pay
Even if you delay
Accepting what I say

Understand I can be your way

I'm willing to take your demand
I've tried to live without you
And I know you'd be better off with another man
A man that could say and make it true

But that's not this lover's way
All I can say is I'd be nothing without you
So don't make it come true today
And prove we're everything as two

Buried as a man
In a lover's quicksand
Do tell me you're setting me free
Just tell me that you love me

Cause I'd be nothing without you
Don't make my plea come true
Living my life... Without you

WHAT LITTLE GLORY

What little glory does a follower have
What little glory does a loser relish
What little glory does a life story save
What little glory have leaders who embellish

Is it dependent upon the time you take
The friends you make
The principles you forsake
Just so you can partake

In the shallow grave of Glory… Or is it

To be righteous courteous studious
And gracious to those who are suspicious
To help them believe it's true
That life's small glories into mountains grew

For the start of the harvest comes from the planting
Of a tiny seed not a large ego's greed
Not from the desires for glory
While no such story… were told recanting

For those looking for more glory
Not the guiding light to man
To do it for the right stand
By committing to a better story

For unselfish reasons
Attempting to cultivate during all seasons
Ignoring snow during the Spring
When the mating birds sing

As the time for preparing the ground
That sunshine surely has found
Turning the soil to multiply the pound
Into thousands in the nest go round

To rise up in the summer
Growing tall and majestic
A model to be a comer
Glory be to the committed heretic

Who cultivates in the fall
As the most glorious day to restore
So that little glory shall be more
Than no glory at all

Because the winter
Brings no glory to the crop
It's post cultivation as the dissenter
That grows glory when the seed again will drop

Into Mother Nature's plot
From the smallest seed we adopt
The glory of the harvested crop
And greed for glory's sake can stop

THE BIRTHING OF THE NATION

THE BIRTHING OF THE NATION

Family life is the birthing of a nation
Pope Francis made the point
That family is the birthing of the nation
Does this define marriage or is it a metaphor
Does it open or close a door

Of course the church defines marriage
As a man and a woman
Of a priest and Jesus
As an immaculate birth
Of Joseph and Mary

Of course same sex defines marriage
As a right to collaborate with another
As a man and queen
As a king and a woman
As a man and a man
As woman and a woman

But the difference is birthing of a family
There can be a surrogate
There can be adoption
There can be fostering
There can be insemination (invitro)

The birthing of a nation
Whether immaculate or collaboration
Or the conventional conception
Or the use of adoption
It results in a family unit
Unless there is contraception

If I were the Pope
There are other convention(s)
Test tube injection
Petri dish fornication
Stem cell transmission
Artificial insemination
DNA formation
Cloning donation
3D printers duplication
Which may need rejection

But he says life at any level is sacred
The sperm and the egg joined is life
And cannot fall to the knife
Cannot protect the youth incest or wife
Even man made strife

Whether you agree or disagree
Speech and behavior is still free
Until it affects me
Until my life is in jeopardy

Then life that starts with tragedy
May not be a sanctity
It's something to which
We will never agree

Reality looks at what was
It's not what a man says
And what he prays
But what he does

That's why the Pope has
Heaven and Hell birthing justice

That may well be an injustice to the unwanted child

IN MY WILDEST DREAMS

I'd thought I'd seen almost everything
I'd thought I'd heard whatever needed to be heard
Not in my wildest dreams
Did I think I'd ever heard
A lovelier word

When you said that our lives are forever linked
By our dreams and hopes coming true
I thought and thought until I couldn't think
Why I didn't know and then misconstrue

I thought I knew most of what I should know
But let me tell you
I thought I'd been almost everywhere
You laid my soul bare

When you held me and said
Don't ever let me leave our bed
Not in my wildest dreams
Did I feel such security that redeems

For true love is more than it seems

I thought I'd had about every thrill
To be offered or start
But I can't explain how you fill
That opening in my heart

When my eyes said I love you
Over and over again
Not in my wildest dreams
Did I expect sex without sin

For most times love is what you read about
Now there's no if ands or buts in retreat
Some silly plot and shallow feelings to flout
True love is hard to repeat

Not in my wildest dreams
Could this old man feel brand new
That love is what it seems
From a lie turning out to be true

With love linking our dreams

THE TIME HAD COME

The time had come for me to realize
That I was done
I could no longer rationalize
The time had come

I had truly hit bottom
I had been stripped alone
I had been torn down to the very basic
Bag of bones

I had been destroyed
By sticks and stones
I was hurt by the words of others
I was cut by the swords of brothers

This may sound remote
Or may even sound dumb
That I would gloat
About having to succumb

But the time had come
And it turned out to be the best
For when the day is done
It's time to take a rest

Time to contemplate
Time to lay back and regenerate
Time to re-trait
If you want heaven to wait

As it resides in front of me
With the bad wind behind my sails
Pushing me toward to the sea of Galilee
In the wake of learning what fails

It's human to regret
For losing that last venture
But you don't win unless you bet
And benefit on experienced adventure

And I don't thrive well as an indenture
Being a risk taking creature
Believing that I am the future
Never can be done challenges are my suture

And I have been hurt
By the enterprise wheel turning
On me by not knowing when to avert
The open sea as the ship is burning

Navigating the storms and nor'easters
Takes a tachometer speedometer
Thermometer barometer odometer
Showing me the way out of goal beaters

Eating away at my working capital
Leaving me short of cash
Then the ship stood still
While I lost the battle

Renovating the assets I have
Making something out of little
Then the business was what I could save
Getting rid of the mistakes made brittle

Yes the time has come
For me to practice what I've learned
As now the success is the sum
Of what you create and have earned

With heaven waiting as my ship turned

INFLATION AND STAGNATION

Inflation
(paying more and getting less)
I see it when I pass the gas station
I see it when I get my spendable ration
I see it when I read about the nation

Inflation
I can't view it with elation
Nor can I understand its creation
But I'm suffering from its impregnation

Inflation
They say it's an expectant economies gestation
A dollar chasing frustration
And government's spending sensation

Inflation
Maybe it's just a result of my faulty expectation
That my welfare comes before excess taxation
And my personal acts don't contribute to stagnation

Inflation really is
A pregnant economy due to excess consumption
And not managing the business gestation
With a buying and borrowing obsession

Which means it's our personal responsibility to manage
Our business and affairs for maximum return
So government doesn't destroy initiative
Just for what we earn

Stagnation
(spending less and getting less quality)
Is when the government gives away too much
Controls lives with a tax crunch
Telling everyone what they should eat at lunch
And run everything on an academic hunch

That government jobs make GDP grow
Even though it adds nothing to cash flow

Deflation

Growth is bad
Nominal
Profits

Good God
Dollar
Plunging

Deflation is primarily due to the Federal Reserve monetary policies
And interference with member bank discount rates
Stagnation is when debt service becomes an excessive burden
On the cost of producing products and services for a profit

Inflation stagnation deflation
The death of a nation
A time to do a reorganization
Elect someone with a business reputation

HIGH ON LIFE

I'm high on life
Give me more
Give me an encore
And I will soar

Higher than I've been before
Higher than the buzz of booze
Higher than the best of news
To the point I'll never lose

This natural high you can't buy
Just enough to smile and fly
Never too old or afraid to die
Just a deeper sigh for life

Oh so high
More than money can buy
I'm high on life
With destiny and my wife

On the wings of my children
I shall ever win
Eternal life with one more grin

Thoughts that are meant to lose
Get lost in booze
Never enjoying nor
Employing good news

The will to avoid sin that lingers
Is within reach my friend
Just take it in your fingers
Be quick
For haste is the trick

As opportunity never lingers
If it slips through your fingers
And you miss this high on life
Yes it's my high on life

Creating prosperity from strife
Making love with your wife
It's never as good
As you think it should

Until you realize
That true love is
The highs above the lows
Over which only regret blows

Give me life
Give me that natural high
Looking up instead of down
Seeking wealth to be found
By turning lows around

Making music from a sound
And building heaven
On the ground
The High Life

Yes I'm high
For happiness shall never die
When you look at today
In the proverbial eye

And tomorrow as just another high

REASON OR RESULT

Am I the reason for or the result of your love
Many rhymes have no reason
Many faults have no result
As when rhymes become reason

When faults become the result of unhappiness
Then there's no reason to make love the result
For the result is the reason
To love me

And believe me I don't mind being used
In a general sort of way
Honey that's a worthwhile price to pay
Especially when I can smile
Sit back and relax a little while

After looking for sympathy
Security and the simplicity of friendship
But don't get me wrong
Please don't string me along

Making me think I'm the reason
Rather than the result
Of your love

Don't give me a cheek instead of a kiss
It's like when I was a child
And my mother gave me a shove
Instead of a hug

And a childhood I don't think I'll ever miss
Of course I can say these are a result
Of her faults
And I'm the product of my environment

And in the meanwhile
Overlook my faults
As being hers
But as certainly as the kitten purrs

If I can't now love
And make rhymes out of reason
And results out of my faults
Then who I am

Am I a real person
Or just a mummy
Blaming my mommy
For being her not me

So if I'm not the reason for your love
And sympathy will make you feel better
So be it
Just don't string me along

Don't you see it's me
Writing this clever simile
With my faults crying out
About no love from my mommy

When in reality I have your love
As the reason for our great family
As the result
Of my mommy having me

Just grow up and be happy Jerry

IN MY BLOOD

You touched me
And I felt warmth
You listened to me
And I felt relieved

You talked to me
And I felt secure
You took me
And I felt you in my blood

Deep down inside of me
That's where you've got to be
For each time I think of you
I'm not in control of what I do

And my time seems to have value
The more you're in my blood
You took me away from loneliness
You showed me how to be a lover

Then I began to discover
I had you in my soul
You set me aside
From my lonely toll

Building me up became your goal
And you told me more than once
With the look and feel of you
That my blood runs true

The more I wanted you
I really didn't care
If you're always there
Telling me who I am

I shall understand
That you're in my blood
Flowing through my heart
Bleeding true into you

Heart mates through and through

DREAMS BECOME REALITY

Visions take on form
Like images in a storm
And dreams become reality
Taken from inside of you and me

Dreams are full of irony
Mortal beings wondering why
The goal of life is to learn to be free
To pursue health and happiness each day

Touch your toes and tell me if I stray
There are no easy lessons
There are no gentle seasons
There are no foregone reasons

When it comes to dreams sought
You should use vision of the mind to see
So it's not caught by
Obstacles from behind reality

Often times in my rhymes
I'm looking for the answer to the evermore
And when I find it beyond the spirit
Laid in the chest of the very best

And on the wings of an angel
Fed by the roots of the clan
Such a feeling tells us
Where creatures stand

They know how to accept reality
They know what is… is what you see
But that hopes come from the dreams
Not fearsome reality

So If you are about wanting to see
Paths and answers
In divinity
Dreams shall deceive thee

But if you treat hopes as already
Being fact
Your heart and soul
Will most certainly accomplish that goal

We as mindful humans are goal seeking
And advancement and evolution
Come not from an institution
But from our intuition

To make our own reality
With thought and prayer
Our destination is finding our dare
By going there

Where reality is but a dream come true

TO SERVE

To serve is to give
To give is to deserve the right
To get
To get is the fulfillment for the moment

No other law of nature is more profound
Not even thunder and lightning sound
Can override the words of God
Saying to serve is to deserve

Saying be aware show you care
That will with faith in kind
Bless you tomorrow
Give you peace of mind

And no woes to sorrow
To serve is the willingness to take a risk
To invest your time and patience
And believe success does exist

So pick your path to service
Put your time into that commitment
Give it your all for better or worse
Feeling the wisdom to wit it's sent

As a giving passenger
Serving the good ship Earth
Navigating the perils
Of giving birth to the Kingdom

With storms upon the horizon
When all is said and done
You have served
And then you've won

The right to sit next to the throne
Not alone
With the maker
As your widow maker

With the blessing of life's undertaker

THE LOVE I HAVE

The love I have for my son
I can feel when he's near me
For the love I have for my daughters
Isn't something you can see
For the love I have for my wife
Has been there for all my life

When they're near me
I know what it's to belong
I know what it's to be needed
I now know fright from strong
And the thrill of a loving seed

Growing inside of me
Growing love's infinity
I have nurtured love
I have these feelings deep
It's the emotion welling up in me
That makes me want to weep

Tears of joy for that little boy
Those wet pearls
For my little girls
And a warmth to life
For my caring wife
I have received love

How lucky I am
A happy peaceful man
That I really haven't always been
I had my times and unhappiness with sin
And I never care to go there again

Nor will I have to worry and
Hurry to nowhere
For I have become love
To those who are always there

For the love I have

WE ALL COME FROM THE SAME SEED

What is your religion
What is your creed
What is your pleasure
What is your need

Ironically for all our greed
We all come from the same seed
To that the Pope decreed
Let's do our duty and good deed

Despite doubts and theories
It's certainly true
We are all on the same God's ferries
Going to the same place with the same crew

By solving the world problems
Not at the warlord whims
But the work for which peace stems
Stemming the loss of human limbs

Slowing the extremism for war
With fear as it's weapon
Using the backs of the weak and poor
As the victims of their counterfeit form of Islam

For the jihad embezzled by ISSI
From the Koran and Mohammad
We face another attack on peace
By a terror group pursuing everything bad

A war or struggle against nonbelievers
Has used the Jihad to bury the principles
Of Islamic pursuit for peace to the disbelievers
And the United Nations must put an end to these disciples

Of fear death and ill will to the preservation of the world
It isn't only the fight of America to protect Israel
It is a nonreligious crusade to make the black flag of ISIS unfurled
As the Pope urged that the coalition of the peaceful nations to fulfill

Before further 9/11's occur
And Syria is such
The wound and the crutch
For a world war three we must defer

For the opportunity to make peace the mission
And the secession of war as the solution to religious differences
So reason minus religion = resolution
To bring the world to its senses

For it will fall without peace and good will to all
The seed will cease

CIERZO (THE WIND)

Cierzo (sirezo) is a strong dry and usually cold wind that blows from the North or Northwest through the regions of Aragon, La Rioja and Navarra in the Ebro valley in Spain. It takes place when there is an anticyclone in the Bay of Biscay and an low-pressure area in the Mediterranean Sea

Cieroz the Wind
The ceaseless
Action of the spirit
Blows where it will

While the trees
Of time
Desire to be still
Fighting back the storm

And Cierzo continues
To blow
With the desire
To change today

Looking to the future
For it must be taken
As we live
Despite being awaken

There the rest
Of our lives
The answer from Cierzo the dry wind
Is blowing again in Spain

The answer is in
Cierzo the Wind
Its relentless power
Predicting a stronger shower

Simple as the Cierzo rain
Emerging from the dry wind
As a cleansing of the earth
Increasing its productive worth

Complex as the Cierzo cyclone
Forming in the dry wind
As white Knights marching
Towards temples arching

Memorable as the Cierzo sun
Warming with a dry breeze
And melting the pressure
While its wind continues to blow

Irony as the Cierzo moon
Freezing the dry ground
By icing the rain
Over the good earth's pain

And still Cierzo reins
Even when Cierzo wains
Cierzo gains
Cierzo is the passing of mortal remains

As Cierzo the dry wind sustains
The Good Earth

INNER PERSUASION

INNER PERSUASION

I've been persuaded by time by love by work by self
And my imagination to avoid what's wrong
... but no magnet could be quite so strong
As a headlong plunge into the icy waters of enterprise
Which after scars, tears and very few cheers,
I became wise

Let me give you some of that wisdom of 60 years
Caught up in the invasion
Of the bottomless pit
Called imagination's persuasion
And the loss of wit

I set out to prove that risk was a lie
It was persistence, attitude, hard work which could defy
The pressure of doubt, indecision,
Which were bigger than I
As I found this out
Too late to deal with life's reason

Well, I'm going to confess
That after 60 years of stress
Working smarter is better than a fast starter
With preplanned steps, conceived by practical reps
Too forestall missteps

To the tune of effective leadership
And not the croon of let's shoot the moon....
Cause emotion and a loose lip brings out the whip
When things go wrong, and they will before long
Persuaded by a sinking ship

Never fear but be prepared
To risk your beliefs so dear
Yes, it is truly an invasion
That imagination's persuasion
Is always, threatening self-preservation

And the strength of heart
Will overcome the failure
To start
Slowing the Universal soul
Begetting the Galactic foal

For then the death of oneness
Will overcome the ignorance
And the stress
Of the Father's son
Being the earth's caress

It's the fear we must address
That we are mere specks
Upon the universal board of chess
And pawns upon its decks

When we humans are the very
Energy that creates
Material images as the corollary
To all of time's transcendent states

While our maker waits at the gates
Weighing an occasion
That results from our inner persuasion
Rewarding an intrusion
That results from our outer conclusion

EVOLUTION

Evolution is no more than a problem
Without a solution
So we will call it an issue
And together cry into a tissue

Politicians have taught us well
That issues are for compromise
And problems cannot be solved
Unless money is involved

But in the parlance of common sense
Avoiding the problem
Makes dollars out of good cents
Amounting to losses in the pursuit of them

Attorneys physicians celebrities one and all
Politicians bureaucrats socialists Fascists
Won't take the ball
Nor the blame just desist

The word issue has become
The most used word in the American culture
Leaving us all deaf and dumb
To life limb and vulture

Rather than confront a problem
With honesty and integrity
Without doubt and sin
Our society is denying reality

Convincing one and another
That problems don't exist
Only between sister and brother
And the solution then does not persist

We can coexist
With our natural inclination
To confront a contest
And take down a threat to our nation

So why do we let the intellectuals
Take away our passion
While stealing from the fools
Their only real wisdom

Truth is in the waning light
It's there in the dark corner
Of our mind's sight
Waiting for our little Jack Horner

Who will lead us out of stupidity
Giving guidance for the answers we elect
To questions that mean something
Attacked without being politically correct

It's not a run-a-round to confuse
If we confront the problem
And not consider the issue
As a fact we can never redeem

For confusion is a tactic
To avoid the responsibility
To act
In all sincerity

An honest solution to the problem
Should be an issue for the greater good

THE MOMENT OF LOVE

My children asked me "Dad"
Tell us what is love
Is it like the hugs we've had
Or just a pull instead of a shove

My children "It's kind of like the moment
You open your eyes at dawn
And get all your wishes sent
After all hopes are gone"

The moment of love is mine
It's yours it's ours
It's everything to find
Like bees mating flowers

It's the moment you first realize
And have eyes for someone that grows
Beyond the normal size
As only the heart knows

And I take you for better or worse

For us it was the moment your mom
Decided it was me… for
Her pulse she could not calm
And she said I do for evermore

It was the moment we first realized
That our minds were in sync
And soothed by our pride
Despite boyfriends I hood winked

That was the moment I decided
I also needed the relief
Of knowing my feelings weren't one sided
As your mom assured my belief

When she said I do for better or worse

It was the moment we vitalized
Our blood to boiling
New stimulation as insecurity died
In the warmth of each-others recoiling

Though our honeymoon was cut short
Our love has never to abort
The moments of love mating together
Birthing three sisters and a brother

So my children when you get
An undying desire for another
And become one with no regret
Tis marriage of a father to a mother

As I have in your Mother's heart
Till death do us part

TALK IS CHEAP

Tell me what I want to hear
Come closer and whisper in my ear
Because what you gotta say
And what you're going
To tell me tomorrow about today

Won't let either of us sleep
Because talk is cheap
It's what you do that will count
As much as the side upon which you mount

For no horse will rear
'Nor will I hear
Something from the wrong side
Whether you've lied or it's just my pride

Unless there's some substance to keep
Good old jawboning is cheap
But if you continually tell me no lies
And you can look me in the eyes

And come across as honest as the day is long
Then how can anything right be wrong
Particularly when you say it's true
And I believe in you

Honesty is the best policy of water deep
Leveling the moat so it doesn't peak
And I don't have to feel the urge to leap
Suspecting your talk is cheap

Make believe
And the will to deceive
Are marks of a character weak
And no wealth to seek

So come one come all
To my speech
Hear my message call
For those I can reach

Aren't holding false witness
Nor telling false hoods
Because words don't dismiss
That talk is always cheap if truth is remiss

Tell me it isn't so before you go do what you dismiss

SEASONS WITH YOU

I've seen the seasons with you
Winter spring summer fall
We've seen them all
Together in all sorts of weather

I've turned the passages with you
Looking up and down
Moving all-around our young pain
For the love we've finally found
Together in the snow and rain

I've watched the falling snow with you
Soundless dots upon the window
I've felt that lover's pain with you
We've made it together as we go

Forming our plans upon the grass
We've watched spring pass
Together we've felt the summer stage
Blowing through our heritage

You're so fair
We've found the magic there
Together holding each other
I've felt the leaves falling to earth
As you looked at me to smother

Tears formed as a autumn freeze
Till I couldn't see
As you said goodbye
To the winter season and me

In spite of the years past
None can retrieve what decisions cast
As the winter of our lives
Cannot in itself do what love revives

If only I had noticed cloudy skies
In your stormy eyes

THE LOOK OF LOVE

Have you ever noticed a mother's face
As a babe lays in her arms
Swaddling's in lace

Have you noticed how her face softens
And her eyes glisten
It's not often that she's not poised to listen

Have you noticed her arms loosen
And as she holds the baby to her breast
It's as if her whole body becomes a nest

Have you noticed her mouth moisten
And pray as if the offspring is a gift
And it's Christmas in her manger's rift

Have you ever noticed when the lovers meet
They seem to come together in subtle retreat
Like quill to a feather penning a love letter

Have you ever noticed the wagging of a tail
When man's best friend hears his master's wail
Leaping to the defense of the holy grail

Have you ever noticed the fluttering of your heart
Without any other reason than her beauty
With your eyes holding to that love tart

Mothers lovers sisters brothers
Have you noticed the bond they have
Connected by the look of love

Eyes glisten
Arms loosen
Mouths moisten
Words form a grail
So beauty can form

A bond called
The look of love

CHICKEN LITTLE'S THREAT

It was a day that Chicken Little had seen
A falling sky
And the wind was mean
Howling out its final reply

The stage was bare
Looking up I saw the curtain come down
The sun had set on it there
And the crowd was nowhere to be found

For the shore was no longer wet
The day was done
And the Kingdom had come
FE fi fo fum the night has won

A-bomb has come
I looked up and the sky was dark
The air was still wiping out the sun
By the wings of that metal lark

Chick Little words I heard
Were being carried from the beaks of a bird
Flying high flying low
Flying around what we already know

For the weapons we stored with faith
Had done it all
The system was said to be fail-safe
But the meltdown proved no one can prevent the fall

It took just one missile moving
Scanning the skies clean
To set the radar into its mode behooving
What Chicken Little had seen

The falling sky with metal birds that fly
Due to the slipping of a thumb
On the trigger of that missile's outrigger
Holocaust had come

But oh so much bigger
That held the payload estopped
Took off before it could be stopped
Leaving behind the controls an A-bomb is dropped

Into its fatal pattern
Circling to kill even the rings of Saturn
Moving oh relentlessly on
I looked up to see the destruction of the dawn

And then it was
The flash blotted the sun
As judgement day does
Chicken Little's threat had come

As I looked up
The curtain came down
The silence was there after the sound
And the reasons for peace too late were found

While Chicken Little's threat did abound

I THOUGHT I KNEW YOU

I thought I knew you
Until you said we're through

I used to hold your hand
Kiss your neck in the car
And take you
To the beating of my desire

I touched you
For the thrill
Afraid to let you go
When my desire wouldn't still

You seemed to understand
As much as I needed you
But I seemed to demand
More than you could do

As the time wore on
Till the thrill
Couldn't overcome
The thoughts we couldn't still

I thought I knew with touch
How to love you
But I found I asked too much
And gave you little too

Not thinking of what's instore
As mine and a part of me
You wanted more
You wanted to be free

I thought I knew
But you proved me wrong
How not to love you
You knew it all along

As bad blood is too strong
So my awakening came
When you walked along
The path of half the game

To get the other half
With me doing as you say
Requires a new path
It was going to be your way

I thought I knew you
And I even said okay
Until you said we're through
Now we'll do it your way

LOVE'S INCISIONS

Some people only think of themselves
Self-indulgence is their drumbeat
Others are in and out of swales
As their mood invites defeat

But the equalizer for that foe
Is the healing of love's incisions
That humbles the largest ego
As it destroys the strongest inhibitions

And wipes away the tears of most fears
Hallowed be the unselfish urge to love
By two people accepting tears
If they can fit each other's glove

And rejecting selfish urge that burns
Selflessness for the loneliness of one
Thinking in only selfish terms
Expecting warmth only from the sun

Which commitment usually affirms
But for many reality does awaken
To the mortal fact
That unto themselves promiscuity is taken

Since to themselves they are vain
For the lonely heal no love incisions
Racked with rejection's pain
From self-imposed decisions

Suffering from feelings that wane
Forsaken by self for another
Then and only then shall a man be sane
From the essence of loving the other

Like the unselfish warmth of his loving mother

MY HEART TELLS NO LIES

I can fake a smile
Close my eyes
Look in style
But my heart can tell no lies

I can play charades
And hide out of sight
But you know as the surface fades
There's only one thing that's right

Created by the right circumstances
And the clearing skies
Truth of our romances
Is that my heart never lies

Yes its rhythm knows
It knows yes it bestows
With its harmony
The melody and the prose

The whetting as the blood flows
And the tingling of the toes
From whence truth bestows
Yes the heart always knows

I can tell a fib or two
And get nothing from the truth
But I can't fib to you
For I've loved you since youth

I used to try to fake it
And let you know I didn't care
But I never seem to make it
Beyond your loving stare

I've melted like an icicle
Held between you and the sun
Wielded for being fickle
Whose days of will are done

As strange as it may be
I really relish the prize
That most can't see
A heart which never lies

For truth is the center of our lives

LIFE'S CLIMB

LIFE'S CLIMB

Someone asked me the other day
What keeps you going
For the price you're having to pay
Life is for deploying not employing

I sat down for the first time
Contemplating the value
Of making my life's climb
Remembering the dime is you

I've said life isn't too much a skit
Different than words when they fit
So definition doesn't mean a lick
When they don't make sweet music

Say it isn't so
Such as befitting yes and a befallen no
They create a safe haven for nonsense
Horse sense or even common sense

Someone asked me the other day
Is it the banker who banks on life
Who really determines what you will say
Or is it the girl you ask to be your wife

Is it the wielder of the cutting ruthless knife
My answer was no bargain either
It's the devil riding the coolly of strife
Or what you'd call a reverent bartender

It's my insidious opinion
Man decides his own destiny
Each is his own imminent domain
Waging his own fate for a sixpenny

His own token becomes the rate
Whether he will negotiate
With the future and fate
Or let now dictate

Finally it's the mean of one
Scene after scene
Waiting to be played
Regardless of who has paid
In between

Someone asked me the other day
Can you tell me what I'll have to pay
And painted a cloudy sky
Wagering future with nowhere to fly

Then I stated the cost of life's climb

Wager life for a penny
And you won't win many
Wager life for a good time
And you will forfeit each dime

Until the sky clears for another climb
Where wagering effort for results rhyme

DESTINY

If you're going to ask me about your destiny
You'd better put a steady hand on your swing
Because you can't blame me
For your failure to act when bells ring

Regardless of who is good
It's all an individual plot
And whether he can or could
Each person gets what they got

Just get right off my back
And get back in your own track
For I'm only responsible for me
And your own reticence fits you like a tee

For help is one thing
And for that thing you can carry on
But Good Samaritan's don't bring
Awakening to the coming of the dawn

And the breaking of the pawn
With habits to be broken
Hoping individual gravity isn't gone
And the future isn't just a token

A turtle can right itself
By turning over in a new space
An elephant can feed itself
By finding a new feeding place

While a human being
Can only right his self
And feed himself
By being sure of oneself

Picking up on his past
Where he didn't go
And couldn't cast
That pursuit is to know

Destiny is what you sow

BORN TO BE EQUAL

How can you divide capital
Into equal pieces for all
And receive more from the same
Who don't multiply or add to the game

Though you may be bright
Come on don't you see the light
We're all not to have the same
Life isn't a silly ballgame

Profits are only the score
The bottom line is just numbers
Even the thief and whore
Have to count up their blunders

Profit have you ever tried to stop it
Have you ever tried to say
It's no good
Have you ever tried to burn petrified wood

Profit many people do try to stop it
They put it down
They say it's no good
To be happier than anyone should

For everybody should be the same
Take those goals away from the game
And hand out everybody their share
Shame… don't you dare

When your brother is going downhill
Even though he doesn't have any will
That it isn't fair
Don't you care

He didn't have the same chance you did
You lucky kid
Just because you worked hard
And your butt is scarred

Doesn't mean you should have more than your brother
More beans means you don't love another
More profit means you're happier than him
That makes his prospects slim

We've got to do away with have and the have nots
The aspiration and the drawing of lots
We've got to be a great society
We've got to exemplify parity

And split up the earth's blackest sod
Then when nothing seems to fit
Under the guise of the wish of God
We'll decide to again pursue profit

Among all us children of God
Tear down that dirty word
Called profit
The only profit we want
Is the one that expounds the ideology
Of total equality

For we were born equal
And to be equal shall be the sequel
To the destruction of profit
Stop it and we all then shall be equal

We all shall seek the same level
Into the doldrums of mediocracy
Our routes shall take the same bevel
Into the bowels of untrue democracy

Into the waste of what used to be
Profit sure you can stop it
You should kill it
You can unwill it

But for such an act begs
And we will pay the price
Even the dogs will stand on their hind legs
And ask for equal rights

For we are all born equal
And to be equal
We must celebrate the death of profit
And the day that profit is dead

Paint us all a communist red

So don't you dare say ifs and buts
That with the opportunity to be equal
Only BIRTH warrants results
And acknowledge we are born with good will

When opportunity is the ingredient
And effort is the quotient of the real
Equality and the right to be free
So give me liberty to be me

What makes America great
Is it's individual creative endeavors
With the good grace of fate
And the dealing of multiple flavors

Equal Is the merit of an education
The pursuit of excellence
By taking a chance
Capitalizing on life's romance

All a result of unequal effort
With unequal talent
With equal opportunities pursued
With equal dissent
With unequal profit to all

How can you divide the capital
Into equal pieces for all
And receive more from the same
Who don't multiply or add to the game

Profits are principles of freedom
We are free to fail
We are free to overcome
Nothing else is totally equal

Without me being me
Profitably

PERFECT LOVE

God loves his children religiously
Mother loves her children warmly
Father loves his children openly
So why can't you make love to me

Come on take me by the hand
I won't hurt you
Don't you understand
There's no perfect love

Mama told me
Take girls by the hand
Take them along
To the Promise Land

Mama told me never
To take girls to bed
Take them by the hand but
Love making is for the honey moon instead

God loves his children not a few
Mother loves her children true
Father loves his children too
So why can't I make love to you

Don't say you're virgin bred
I've been misled
Come on… to thee I wed
So we can go to bed

You told me you love children
Even though that be true
Giving up your body isn't a sin
After you say I do

Sex isn't easy to every one
And loyalty isn't free
Without a daughter or son
There's no perfect family

God loves our children
As a Father I love his children too
As a Mother your physical love is no sin
So make our perfect love come true

Then God loves me and you

HALFTIME

Football has a halftime
Basketball has a halftime
Rugby has a halftime
Taking time out for a turnabout

Take a breath
The beat of the music tolled
Through my head
And your pillow was still laying
Upon my bed

All I could think of
All I could dream of
Was how we fell in and out of love
The mystic and all good senses
Said we were the prince and princess

Everyone quite naturally held us in awe
Never guessing
Our love would thaw
Though the ruse is never told
The actors act by some mold

And if by some quirk or suggestion
One or the other looks for reflection
Leaving dissection
In the search for perfection

About the why and wherefore
That which was once a thrill
Becomes a bore
And true affection will be caught
In the closing door

Now if we could have called time out
We could have probably gotten back together
And had halftime rather than a bout
Having weathered that stormy weather

So regret is beating in my head
I wonder yes I wonder
As I feel the loneliness of being alone in bed
If my pain will turn off this blunder

Injured and doing rope a dope
I seem to be going down for the last time
With my inability to cope
Having lost you without a half time

By not taking time out for a turnabout

CAR SICK

Did you ever ride in the back of a car
And had to sit there
Much too far
With a boring stare

Saying "Aren't we there"

First you become uneasy
And then a little queasy
Mama called it taking a lick
But I call it car sick

"I have to pee"

And it's no news about what I say
If you're in my shoes
Driving all day
With the car sick blues

"I'm thirsty and hungry"

Just something from the cupboard
You'd be car sick too
With old mother Hubbard
Stuck in your shoe

"I don't feel good"

With this traveling man
Moving on down this two lane road
Thinking and singing to my van
Quieting those kids I have stowed

"I'm on the road again"

With Willie Nelson keeping me awake
And my past pushing on the brake
Hoping my life isn't at stake
Someone said it must be fate

"Pull over and take a break"

And though this may not come as any news
Just try breaking the car sick blues
Cause as a man when there's no choice
You can bitch and moan and raise your voice

"raise it and sing the car sick blues"

But when you have no other life to choose
You're going to have to learn more
Than singing the car sick blues
By holding the hammer to the floor

"Move over rover I'm coming through"

Grinding the wheel 'til my knuckles turn blue
Squinting my eyes against the glaring hue
Nothing more to say or do
Than to wonder what I'm getting into

"Look out I'm coming through"

And though it may be a loose lip
Just like when we're a kid
We become what we did
As Mama let it slip

"About the next trip"

Sitting in the backseat
Tummy turning over and over again
With itchy feet
Still believing that a four leaf clover will win

"And lotto is a sin"

Just waiting for us
To have our number a pick
Even though we make a fuss
No way are we going to be nibble or quick

"Come on boys don't be sick"

"We're almost home"
Mama said like some hick
"Only losers bitch and moan"
"Buckle up and wait a lick"

"There at last we're there at last"

Mama this casino is a blast
Using power ball as a quick pick
Will we win never again harassed
By being car sick

I BELIEVE

I believe in tomorrow
Though it sometimes
Seems far far away
I believe in yesterday
Though it sometimes
Seems to melt away

With aging the price to pay

I believe in love
Though it sometimes
Seems it's something I can't say
I believe in heaven
Though it sometimes
Seems Hell's in the way

And fear is here to stay

I believe in God
Though it sometimes
Seems doubt came to stay
And I believe in today
Though it sometimes
Seems I've forgotten how to pray

About love and the fruits of play

I believe in work
Though sometimes it will dominate
When it should substantiate
Though it sometimes
Seems destiny and fate
Will inspire us to create

And everything else can wait
Amen

GIFTS

Give me nothing to work for
And I will give you nothing

Give me something to work for
And I will give you everything

Give me foresight to do better
Give hindsight to do no worse

Give me insight to do good
Give me far sight to see a curse

Give me something to die for
And I will give you my life

Give me a reason to live
So I can love my wife

It's these gifts that state
That I am a gift to my mate

It's these gifts that create
Our destiny as fate

BOTTOM OF THE DECK

Life can be made up of lies
Ifs and buts and whys
But does it take a real sleuth
To determine the reality of truth

I don't think so
Though some may question my right to know
I think it might be very simple
As basic as a smile and an inherited dimple

It's as basic as being able to
Eliminate what isn't really true
And what's left
Is the depth of the chin's cleft

It's the knowledge and forethought
Borne out by experience's plot
The reality of happiness sadness
Madness and gladness

All left for us to live
Not necessarily for all of us to give
For some have to live with lies
And doubts that ill will epitomize

But truth must be there
It must endure indifference and duress
Giving truth its essence of fair
For without it lurks sin's behest

For a life without lies
And the reason to disguise
The truth would not mean as much
And there would be no warmth in a touch

With it we must live with the sleuth
The uncouth and the doubt of youth
So we can know the power of truth
Body language is telling us the untruth

Simple as a cheek's dimple
On the liar's face
Deft as a chin's cleft
As he draws an ace

From the bottom of the deck

THE CREST

THE CREST

A crest starts with a pebble
And the ripples form from storms
The strength grows unstable
Until the crest forms

As it rolls to shore
It emanates power
Rolling into evermore
From a good rain shower

Twenty pebbles tossed by a fool
Individually form a whirlpool
Of destruction and finality
Taking all out to sea

While twenty pebbles thrown
Creates a tidal wave home grown
With both hands by a gruel
To set the sea into turmoil

But throw twenty pebbles
With the same hands with zest
Creates a wave that will crest
For all to behold as it trebles

A tidal wave of love of old
A condition to have and to hold
Good if put to good sensation
The ripples of procreation

Letting the good apples
Embrace the glue and staples
To go free grudgingly
As ripples into the sea

Twenty ripples cresting
Over our adversity
Handles the whirlpool divesting
Divorce from our anniversary

There is no stopping the wave
The tide and undercurrent
When the strength that we behave
Crest from the vows we do consent

This crest starts with a rebel
And the ripples form from scorns
The strength grows unstable
Until mortal love forms

A reservoir for the weak and poor

THE WHITES OF THEIR EYES

The whites of their eyes
Twice their size
Turned our attention to the skies
Revealing a sun beginning to rise

A round ball of fire
Could have been the devil's attire
Hidden within a mortal's desire
Swinging between life and death
On a wire

A wire so thin it can't be seen
Cutting off routes where we've been
Trimming the fat till it's almost lean
Coloring the stage for one more scene

Tempered by the liberal tempest
Basking at the table is the best
Rendering defunct all the rest
And flunking those who care to take the test

Again trying to read the whites of their eyes
Ignoring the babies' cries
And wondering if the clown's in disguise
Just to win last prize

While the conservative jester keeps jesting
With the libertarian tester testing
Those considered elite at besting
Are the socialist rest texting

Then God finally said turn over a new leaf
Saying if you have to handle the gravity of grief
I can't just allow you to go where you've been
For I can't see you discarding sin

So that you'll win
In a world of sin
For democracy isn't just a sacrament that flatters
It guarantees all that matters

When sin isn't just a sentiment
Praising each theological impediment
Both are leniently used as liniment
For those sore knees bent for the revenant

Till the Bible is left cracking and closed
Its impurities are exposed
Upon a deliverance that froze
Imposing immunity truth disclosed

As those symbols were put away
Put down with justice to pay
Resting in a dungeon to decay
As politicians delay

Gridlock's use of oratory filibuster
Is correctness for dishonest surmise
Spotting up those who chatter
So democracy dies

Hiding the whites of their eyes

That only a third party denies

DUMPING GROUNDS

Each man must find his dumping ground
A place to shed frustrations doubt and dread
For it's the release of problems and reservations
That can bring you peace instead

Some choose methods that only compound
What they think they'll lose
And their dumping ground
Merely builds up a higher mound

And doesn't decrease
What they need for release
For they usually choose the easy road
Merely shifting from one shoulder to the other their load

Dragging them on till they tire
Misinterpreting the dumping ground for desire
Picking up on perversions of sex and the like
Putting the finger in sanity's dike

As trash builds up
And the land fill says no way
Don't let the miseries fill your cup
Dump them each day

Dumping what they're perceived to be
Obstacles to their own reality
Certainly not dumping it on someone else's ground
Who can't rid it and spreads it all around

So release that frustration
But if it's misconstrued it can turn on you
For sustenance is not moderation
Just like too much food and Mountain dew

So the dumping ground mustn't contaminate
If done for the betterment of creations
Where you've been or where you meditate
Leading to hard earned personal relations

Do it with a song a poem a painting a book
Or with a simple sigh taken before you're mistook
As the lynch pin of being under booked...
And overlooked

For all mankind has found
Bury your doubts by lowering the mound
Of over indulgence that can bring you down
So don't misconstrue your dumping ground

REASON TO CONFESS

Judge Judy ism
"The mess you need to confess"

"I need to know the reason
And an excuse is not the reason"
"The difference is your choice
To try a lie and excuse the mess up
Or fess up
And take responsibility
And it will set you free"

Reason + reality = resolution
Excuse – reason = conviction

You may screw up and are sorry
But not ready to confess
Rather you give a reason
For the mess

When confession is not the problem
But only defers the consequences
By committing the mortal sin
Before you come to your senses

Justifying your action
With an excuse
Is a no win situation
Just avoiding personal abuse

When in effect
This decision is an insightful factor
A dissect
Into your character

This avoidance of the reason
That hangs us all
Really hinges on our decision
To tell a lie and fall

Rather standing tall
And fessing up
Cleanses our deepest pore
And conscience for more

As character walks through the door

MICE AND MEN

Hold my hand and you can have my heart
I know I've confused you many times
Frustrated and verbally abused you
With my lines

Said things I didn't mean
Became distant
And always leaving the scene
Almost like an adolescent

I'm thinking more of appearances
Than I'm thinking about our romances
This is a problem of improper priorities
Like not relating to truth with defenses

Just waiting for it to do so

Because there would be no end to stop
And start of a new relationship too frigid
By cooling of a temper too hot
While softening of a hand held too rigid

A finer tune to the music we're not
But I guarantee you I can make you see
You'll have my heart nonstop
At the roots of a family tree

As a good start you have my word
Bank it and cash it in
Leverage by my soul referred
A love-fest rare among mice and men

Invested in my best friend

THE PILGRIM

I'm just a pilgrim
Looking for love
Beating my drum
That's what I'm thinking of

Do you hear the beat
It's the beating of my heart
And the stomping of my feet
Waiting for my blood to start

I'm a pilgrim
Looking for love
Feeling like I could scream
But cooing like a dove

Just off the boat of loneliness
So long that I must confess
Just a pilgrim in your loveliness
With many more things to assess

Like holding hands
It was just strands of fingers to touch
And those feelings I didn't understand
Didn't mean too much

With no relation to my feelings
Since my pilgrimage came true
For my plans confessed by my kneeling's
I'm no pilgrim with you

Will you marry me

No why… have you turned away
Against our bows and vows
Having burned the bridge
Not finding common ground concerned

Doubt has found its way to your door
Rejecting our future's worth
But retaining what I adore
It's a swaddling boy's rebirth

So my journey will always be
A pilgrimage searching for thee
To have you say happily
Yes to marry me

EYE TO EYE

You turned over and looked me in the eye
It was like sunshine in the morning sky
Your mouth moved to a smile
And I just wanted to lay here by you for awhile

It seemed like we talked all night
Dealt with the gray
Between black and white
Questions like how we pray

How long does love last
Is today going to be lost to our past
Will our time together be cast
Into a future too vast

Like a flywheel
In an old automobile
With nothing to conceal romance
Only function above performance

Then looking each other in the eye
We decided to retreat
Until we want to complete the ride
Right up front not the rumble seat

For love and commitment must grow
It must grow deeper than the ticking of time
Broader than the meaning we can bestow
Putting forth why we humans are like twine

Holding together
In all kinds of weather
Then just looking each other in the eye
Asking why

Why lover's cry
When they no longer see eye to eye

TURN HOMEWARD

My eyes have seen
The beauty of the sunset
My ears have heard between
The singing of the wind and a droning jet

My voice has spoken
The meaning of words
My heart has broken
From the afterwards

My work has turned me down
With the time it took
My plans have turned around
With the dreams I mistook

My dreams squared to round
The future and direction
My fears turned to sound
And tears of elation

My eyes have seen
The beauty of my love
My ears have heard
The singing from above

Singing don't turn back
When you feel alone
You're finding your comfort zone
With a homeward tact

Your eyes will water
And your ears will ring
As a voice will sing
Come see your daughter

Don't feel alone
She's on the telephone

LIFE OF A PUPPET

Life of a puppet
Dancing lightly upon its feet
Puppeteer deftly creating life
With his feat

The puppeteer shall dance his skills
Only if there's compassion
For the puppet's wills
And expression to somehow fashion

A matter of true being
Illustrating the impression
Lifelike of what we are seeing
Though it's an illusion

Of a real person on a wire
If the puppet does cooperate
The puppeteer's desire
We all can't wait

For the next moves will require
To the coordinated command
Otherwise the jumble will sire
Leaping up and failing to stand

Dancing in circles
Round and round
Are just miracles
As the puppet falls down

Getting back up requires
The puppeteer's strings to tension
And the puppet retires
Its apprehension

Tugged each and pulling apart
Then we have a body
Breaking its wooden heart
As the stage is now shoddy

Pulled without discretion
Pushing tugging with dread
The puppet's destination
For the crowd's seeing as if bled

Immolating as the puppet is dead

In the puppet's further strife
For the strings are snarled
The puppeteer takes out his knife
As the puppet loses it world

And its DUMMY life

ODE OF KELLI JO

Hidden beneath the blanket of frost
Lies the greenery some thought lost
Hidden above the clouds so blue
Is the sunshine and days brand new

Wingless but in jest to wrinkles
Riding above the winds that blow
Blond and freckles
The ode of Kelli Jo

She sweeps away
Those sad thoughts of crying
After she is gone don't betray
Her wake is for trying

Bright and love's to dance
Like a bubbling brook
Rushing like is a spring fancy
If you take a look

As her smiles fly
Her days stand up in style
Her attitude won't belie
As she goes the extra mile

Fighting the urge of asking why
Telling us how not how it was
Saying just I'll "do it or die"
Because it means more if she does

Christmas and birthdays are her joy
Held with feeling to decoy
That life isn't a toy
It's that cute neighbor boy

Ah yes you might be coy
That your child shall bestow
Upon every child to live that joy
The ode of Kelli Jo

The truest feelings dear
Our life will love her so
For she shows no outward fear
Only the urge to go go go

Lying below the frost so cold
Is the greenery to have and hold
It just takes sunshine to melt it down
And bring back the princess' crown

I'm writing this so all will know
That frost can melt and go
And green can turn to brown and fold
But Kelli's ode shall never grow old

A song to her mettle gold

LONNIE AND DONNIE

My two cousins Lonnie and Donnie
Were a pair of my kins
Also friends
Some thought them twins

Except history attends
To authorities who knew them to be
Just plain ornery
That was Lonnie and Donnie's only sins

Their mama and papa's regard
Were as good as they could be
When living a life made hard
To overcome incest and poverty

They were on that edge
Of being fed or just plain hungry
Head long into some stage
Of trouble because of skullduggery

As if tomorrow they would be dead
They played life hard
And came away from their scrapes
More and more scarred

They got into what it brought
For they got had bad dreams
Each time it seems they got caught
In the middle of their schemes

Just left holding the bag
As those crazy Dill's did it again
And they got the tag
Right back in jail where they've been

Each one grew up and went their separate ways
They had few ups and mostly downer days
Lonnie he was caught and in and out of jail
And then one day when he couldn't make bail

Along came Uncle Sam with a plan
He went off to Germany land
And learned a trade
Lost an eye the price he paid

Kicked his drinking habit
Happy now a married man
A family and the right to have it
As a winner not an also ran

Above it all
Straight and tall
Donnie on the other hand
Never learned how to land

He flew from one scrape to another
He wasn't as fortunate as his brother
He married and had a family
That only compounded his tragedy

As he climbed in and out of the bottle
His hand was always stuck to the drug throttle
His marriage fell
His life turned to hell

For he threw them in
After thirty years of sin
Drinking and shooting up
No way out no way to win

Which I'm sure most certainly led
To him hanging himself dead
In that cell
That must have felt like the pits of hell

Lonnie and Donnie dear
Tell us about life's deepest fear
That's the days upon end
When your lonely looking for a friend

To give them a sense of responsibility
A sense of direction and security
When it's not there it's only fair to conclude
That fate must most certainly intrude

With Lonnie he caught himself in time
With his wife's help
He overcame his life of crime
Improving his future health

He became a stronger man
With a life of concrete made out of sand
Building homes on his land
A successful businessman

Donnie on the other hand
Couldn't cope
And when he lost hope
He did what he turned do dope

As the chemical pits of hell could
Tell his story not ending good
For the days of Lonnie and Donnie dear
Lived in grief and fear

Could be very near
If your children come from poverty
And you can't teach them love and security
Their life will be of fear and misery

Lonnie kudo's to you
For what the love of work and love could do
And to Donnie's wife and kids condolences
When dad never overcame his offences

And let booze and drugs destroyed his senses

MORALITY

Morality shall God save thee
Or shall the Devil celebrate our mortality
Sin as no moral good
Morality as from within

And making a can from a could
Morality shall man save thee
Selfish thoughts of what feels good
Or shall his weakness cause his mortality

Wishes rather than not
Morality shall man's sense save thee
With wills rather than what I've got
Or shall the deviations inflict mortality

The heart for most a gentle place
Though the ghosts may haunt the inner space
Morality shall faith save thee
Or shall they crucify you into mortality

They the illusive they… the plight of man
Comes what may from his own command
Morality can we save thee
Or shall we create our own mortality

For God sent us morality to have and to hold
And to protect us for eternity
So if we fail the test
With the principles to which we're blessed

Mankind can only confess
We shall be the winners or losers
Of the game of moral chess
Since we are the beggars or choosers

Give us abstinence from immorality… neither gives me immortality

AN EXPRESSION

Love is an expression to another human being
Of all feelings all fears all doubts under the sun
All aspirations all that you're conceiving
An expression that doesn't occur for everyone

It's not as readily obtained as the warmth of the sun
It's illusive for many a mother
And for a few it shall not exist until done
For only those who persist in loving another

Shall know the love of a brother

Some misconstrue infatuation as ultimately true
The love of body is not love's goal
It will not make you whole
For love must capture the soul

It will narrow your focus
To everything meaning the both of us
A true meaning of oneness
In an expression by a kind caress

A quieting of the urge to wander seek and plunder
It's the will to refrain from being selfish and vain
For to serve another before you serve yourself
Is the ultimate expression of love's gain

So if you wonder about your feelings your intentions
Reasons and dissensions
Before your own personal aspirations put those of a mother
And then you will truly love another

As a mother wants for a sister and brother

THE SAME SKY

Why is the same sky blue for some
And before a storm for others
Why is the same day a burden for some
And a wonder for others

Why is the same song abrasive to some
And soothing to others
Why are the same goals a challenge to some
And just roles to others

Why is the same church ringing a chime to some
And demeaning to others
Why is a fairytale a dream to some
And a bore to others

Is it the eyes and ears of the beholder
Or the tastes and wastes of the older
Or the plates and crates of the scolder
Or the strength of the arm and shoulder

Might it be the differences are the same
It's just how we see the playing of the game
For the days of stress and cavort
You have the graphics of life being too short

People are ordinary persons
Doing extraordinary contortions
Thinking it will get them what they want
A name in history or the glitter of a debutante

The reasons most as many as the seasons
But most of the differences are all alike
It's how hard you want to peddle the bike
Because the hole to plug is in the same dike

Challenges and effort are just rules of the game
And though there may be circumstantial differences
The holding of hands just clears the senses
Although it may seem like fruitless pretenses

Just add the individuals to the consequences
By putting them in a group activity
Or into an endless loop
The Star Trek would track the same destiny

Would a social commune eventually kill democracy
So even though equality sometimes is hard
To even halfway know who is dealt the card
It's just as well for well it can be

The answer to what is the color of the same sky
When the only difference being white you and black I
It's the freedom to be free
Extended to you and me

HOME FOR THE HOllDAYS

HOME FOR THE HOLIDAYS

Holidays are a time for relaxation
A mixture of home and self
And a spiritual felling of fulfillment
Patriotism in memorial
Celebration of the harvest
Dedication to a new belief

A new year
A renewed hope
A revitalized will to cope
Home for the holidays

Returns to us in many ways
Our love of family
For our neighbors
And for mankind

If we will only take the time
To bow our heads in humility
In piety in reverence to the will of God
For the chain shall not be broken
And the words shall not be unspoken
As the holiday's moment is more than a token

It's pride and circumstance that we praise on our holidays

CHRISTMAS

The day that Christ was born
Was a day like no other
Until the virgin gave immaculate birth
To the greatest man born on earth

The birth of the savior
The meaning of the new beginning
For sinners and winners
Fault we decay come what may
And are forgiven on the seventh day

The glory of the Holy Ghost
Loving Jesus and us the most
Acting as the overseer and host
To that we give our toast

Bless all those that observe the mass
By the stories of the past
When the Three Wise men did fast
And the light that Star of David cast

Upon an earth enjoined by the Devil's hearth
Only to be cleansed of its girth
By the immaculate birth
Wiping away sins for good's worth

Presents are given as the Sheppard flocks
Hosted the baby Jesus from their stocks
While the threat of Satan mocks
The faith of the Holy Grail's box

Happy merry joyful Christmas
As celebration of the mass
Of the religions flair
All are at attention for Hope is there

And when God looked down on the world
That was now free to hurl
Out the indignant and unfurl
The flags of impunity surreal

In his image the future
Was blessed for those inclined
To love and be kind
As the faith revelation left behind

Praise be to Christmas as the christening of all holidays

CELEBRATING THE NEW YEAR

Closing out the past
And opening the door to the future
Letting the soft cool breeze
Of a new day
Blow across your face
Focusing your eyes
Far off in space
And setting your tracks
Firmly in place
For the sun rises on the horizon
For us to seek
Its beauty
To call us to duty
To set aside our pride
Though it does cleanse us
Like the evening tide
But leaving us refreshed
Restored and ready for the new day
The New Year
The new life we live in the next year
In the vessels of time
That carries us to the brink of the tide
But brings us back to the beach
Partaking in the ultimate goal
That is a reconstituted soul
There is no looking back
Except to holiday memories
No regrets no losing bets beget
The will of dreams and fantasies

So take the New Year by the clock's hand
Follow it along the path you have drawn
And never fear in your mind
The New Year's opportunity shall never be gone
It is waiting for your brain to dawn
While doubt is a servant's pawn
Checkmate you have won the right to spawn
A new way a new plan
Just follow the footsteps in the sand

Praise be the New Year Holiday as it will never end

EASTER

The days after Christ was born
Were no days like no other
For until the virgin gave birth
To the greatest man born on earth

What made men upright
Wasn't the savior's deeds
It was the cultivation of man
Planting in his seeds
Sowed in hearts not for himself
But for mankind
Healing the sick
And sighting the blind

Through his efforts others learned
That taking was to be spurned
Giving was to be earned
And with these words
Christ was destined to fall prey
To the Jackals and Blackbirds
The very ones that needed him the most
They needed to meet the Holy Ghost
And the reasons why
The devil was the meaning of fear to die
But to them this was a threat
And they thought better yet
To quiet this man
To nail his hand
To cut him with their sword
So the threat would disappear
And they could live with their own
Burdensome fear

As the nonbelievers hung him on the cross
No less inclined by His loss
Never thinking never wondering
Why he didn't seem afraid to die
The more at peace he looked
The more the crucifixion crowd
Shivered and shook

He said words they couldn't understand
There were no threats
There was no command
There was just forgiveness in His eyes
In His tone and He didn't seem to be alone
And then in His last gasping breaths
He said "Lord forgive them
They know not what they do
They should be saved and
Not damned by the wrath of you"

Then the sky darkened
The thunder clapped
The lightning struck
And by no mortal plan
Christ' spirit left that land

The fading of the day
Allowed the soldiers to carry Him away
And the silent solitude of the weeping
Tears of gratitude to be buried
In a tomb much colder than the Devil's womb
But lo the light didn't leave the room
As they rolled the rock in place
Blocking the view of the peace on the Savior's face
Those who took vigilance there were few
And kept in place by their need to dare
Damn the memory of what He'd said
That in two days he would rise from the dead
As the time passed by

The thunder and lightening
Crossed the sky
And the eyes began to dry
All that could be heard
Was the jackals' cry

The night turned to day
And no one seemed to care
That the disciples began to gather there
Not knowing why since they'd been afraid
To be with their Christ
When he was crucified to die
They felt this urge to be silent
To be vigilant to believe
That more was to be conceived

And on the third day
After a night of silence
And the setting of peace upon those there
The troops came to check upon the spoils of their game
But when they arrived they found
That a quake had cracked the earth

Without a sound
The rock had been rolled aside
The Mother Mary looked on with pride
And it was now known the Messiah
Had not mortally died
It was in the signs
It was in the faces
It was in the hearts of those standing there
Who all became undoubtingly aware
The presence of eternity
And the omnipotence professed
That be the sanctity
Of the Father whose Son was the Holy Ghost

Praise be the Holiday for life that shall never end

MEMORIAL DAY

Blessings are too few not to be sacred
And to the sacred
We must respect the heritage of the past
Unto those that gave of themselves

For our right to exist beyond D day
Pearl Harbor and Ground Zero
Within the confines of freedom
Within the sanctity of the Constitution
And for the right of every man and woman
To have an equal opportunity
To express his or her thoughts
Her dreams his schemes
Her needs his seeds
Can await us in the future

In a manner that will better humanity
And cure war and corruption of man
Be it the soldiers of the night
The battleground of the day
Or the security that peace abounds
All must be saluted and remembered
All must be held in highest adulation
For it's to those principles
That the preservation of the earth
Has been given birth
And forever shall live
For those that give
Their lives for peace on earth
Good will to men and women
To Give Peace A Chance

Praise be the Veterans' Holiday as our unholy day of war

THE FOURTH OF JULY
INDEPENDENCE DAY

To be free is just thoughtful words
In the minds
Of those who can speak
Who can express their feelings
Without fear or reprisal
Freedom is but a dream
Left not to be taken for granted
To those who live in hunger and fear
Found to be oppressed
For they have no will or redress

Freedom on the other hand
Is constantly on the minds
Of those who have broken through the barrier
Of doubt and fear
Who have broken the bonds
Imposed by themselves
Around their own wills
To be free of fear and war's bondage

Freedom is in the words
Of those who have tasted its joy
Its benefits
Its inspiration to create a better place
So others can attain fulfillment
That is the ultimate grace
So battles have been waged
And wars have been won
For the underlying purpose
Of spreading the message or worth
Of the freedom of Heaven on Earth

Praise be to the Holiday for Peacekeeping Soldiers of the Good Earth
The first responders to protect life limb and liberty

LABOR DAY
HARVEST THE SOUL

Harvest then a time to rest
From hard work then a time to savor
The fruits of the crop's labor
The southern wind that will stop
And the northern winds shall then blow
Until we have snow
But not before we ask
God to restore
The vitality of the land
The repentance of the hand
Tis Labor Day
Let the harvest begin
Tis the time to rest
A rest from life's contest

To always produce more
To rise to heights far above the floor
As labor salutes their score
As management salutes money
And the bees are out of honey
And Americans stand together
Against the enemies of the land
And their enterprise
So open your eyes society
Put away for a day your sobriety
Your prejudices malice's and analysis
For the joy that can be felt
By every girl and boy

That the fruits of man's labor
For the good of oneself and one's neighbor
Shall be the almighty reason
For celebrating
The blessed coming Harvest season

Praise be the Holiday celebrating Mother Nature

THANKSGIVING

The one day when thanks are given
For the fruits of work and family
And the freedom to live our own way
Without obstruction and display
Of power and quest of control
Of our wishes and dreams

Also to recognize how our decedents
Overcame forces of the Kingdom
For the freedom to express thanks
And pray for their own God
In a world that is never at peace
And a future that is in our own reach
And wasteful habits
Waiting for us to be responsible
By conserving our assets and dissolving
Our liabilities for the sake of America's
Great Enterprise and Social Model
For the rest of the world to immolate
If it be their will

Against the will of Dictators
The Lords of War and Fear
In building the infra structure
Attained in America's 200 years of
Implementing a constitution
For the People by the People
And of the People so help us God

So we are thankful for our forefathers
Our leaders of the past
And the leaders of the future
And may they be honored by
Observing this Thanksgiving Day
Our abundance our fortunes
Our obligation to our children
And their siblings to be Peaceful
Keepers of the environment
By conserving and honoring
The salvation of the Good Earth
Amen

As for Columbus Day, Veterans' Day,
Presidents' Day, Martin Luther King Day
Bosses Day, Nurses Day, Election Day, etc.

We recognize our strengths as a nation
Of Holidays and thankful celebrations
For that we are special in our dedication
To all Americans so long as they participate
In the Harvest and fruits of our labor
As a loyal and committed voter

In our democracy of peace makers

STOP FIGHTING LOVE

Stop fighting love
Come home to me
Fly down from above
Where we both can see

What we are fighting so diligently
I think we'll find It most exciting
For love isn't for fighting
Don't fight love

Come home to me
Fly down from above
So we both can see
What we have been fighting so diligently

Sit here beside me
Fold your wings
And look at me
And feel that my heart sings

So we can agree
Please don't fight it
My love is free
Don't fight something you can't see

Come back home and sit with me
For it can be exciting
To take off the chains and let it be
Please stop fighting me

I can see by the slant of your mouth
And by the set of your eyes
That our bird is heading south
To avoid stormy skies

But don't you realize
It's not worth fighting
A true love so exciting
Not a fantasy but inviting

If this seems silly not real
And you're getting a disguise
Let me give you something to feel
Look at my mouth and eyes

It's a look inside my heart
Hoping yours will not part
From a soul mate
Who can't wait

Unless you have another love

Then I will not fight your
Flight to another show and tel
Hoping you will find the door
To a friend as well

MOTHERS AND DAUGHTERS

Kimber Leigh and her mother Shari
Are having trouble meeting what they see
Each is one
And each are they

Bigger than the roles they play
There are reasons for this state
And it has more to do with their past life
Than fate

For coincidence in a more mature sense
Comes from having a grip
On your own personal lip
Not succumbing to its bite
Not being tempted to give in to its spite

For it's the wielding one
Who's day is done
Before it starts
Though it's been dealt a full house of hearts

For it's that daughter
No it's the proven right of a character
That really counts
Not the foal the jockey mounts

Structured on might
It has nothing to do with why Kimber Leigh
And her Mother Shari's individualality
It's about will and feeling free

Both condoned by Mother Shari

Who only wants the best for Kimber Leigh
Back to the reality of what made her free
But she sees in those daughter traits
That her memories abates

It wasn't the simple discipline
Of always being right
It was learning what her mother felt
Learning it good when dealt

The daughter learned it too
But like her Mother Shari
Doesn't yet see what's true
That's the love that others degree

And there lies the burden of an apprentice
Moistened at times by the coolness of her kiss
Mother Shari shows Kimber Leigh a princess
What she cannot miss

Feeling as her Mother Shari wants
To be something she didn't miss
Accepting herself confronts
Life's values to a list

Patience with children
Persistence with work
Fitness with family
Loving sense with mate

And loyalty to self
Made traits

"I always saw my thoughts and temperament in her and I knew instinctively what she was thinking. We are great friends as a result." Her Mother

SIGNS

All along the highway
Look and you shall see
Signs of the times
Stating their decree
While the stars align

No left turns
Stop and yield
Do not pass
Don't exceed the speed limit
Cross at your own risk

Then on the calendar
I'm a Libra
I'm a Sagittarius
I'm a Virgo
I'm Cancer

Then in the skies
It's the falling North star
It's the Haley's comet
It's smoke signals
It's a full moon

Signs can be aboding
To the watchful eye
Or somewhat foreboding
If you're unwilling to try
Twitter and downloading

Watch the signs and you shall see
If you have the courage
To be what you want to be
For hesitation can be the literal cage
Imprisoning us by technology

Breeding the frustration for a man
Who regrets not being a boy
For life has no passerby
It merely has those who are willing to deploy
Signs telling us when not why

Before we die
The signs are there for all to see
We can either follow them
Or fear them indefinitely
Because they lie

Those who shirk and cringe
And never start their work
For yet another binge
Lose momentum and lurk
In the shadows and on the fringe

They shall be the regretful ones
The sons of sons
The daughters of daughters
The losers of losers
The signs of times gone to the choosers

Who then fulfil their own signs
Once hidden by fear and doubt
Found buried in their own past confines
Being a victim rather than a scout

Following the signs of the times
Falsely pursuing Indian smoke signals
Custer lost his last stand
To not being able to understand

Times and signs are disappearing with the smoke

THE GOSPEL SINGER

Massa said "Listen to my words"

There shall be no words in the field
There will be no running words in the huts
There shall be no drums to wield
There shall be no gathering of nigari's

Cept to honor the Seventh Day
This is the law for slaves
You are bonded so do as I say
Heed my overseer's whip for the knaves.

Behold the birth of Gospel as the revelation
by Jesus Chris
That the blacks are the roots of salvation

He said "harken my children find the way
to the promised land thought released
By the words in the voices you pray
Your bonds will be released
By the message your uplifted voices bring
As a gospel to sing"

The Gospel Singer

"No readin' no wrtin' we ain't got no place
No place ta goes face ta face
Nobody knows the troubles we'se seed
Oh lawd save us we gotta be freed

Dat promia land hallelujah we hasta has
Ah souls in de promise land
Tonight dair will be 20 souls comin' hand to hand
Take 'em to yo breast hole 'em close
Causen dey'se gonna board de chariot
Befo' dat roosta' crows

This'ens de way we finds our way
Our ways jes gotta go cain't stay
Up to's de promise land so far away
By de chariot in de sky comeons
Lawd take us dis we prays"

Commentary

On Sunday we sung for Monday
What did we sing and pray
About going North a chance to be free
As we sung our message in melody

Gospel gave us freedom to talk to our brother
About our hopes and prayers for one another
For as Massa beat us down so long
We rose to make our plans by song

Gospel led us to our Promise Land
By way of underground and helping hand
Breaking away from ship and chain
To the North and a different pain

Epilogue

Of slavery oppression and cruelty
We are free of Massa but not society
We're still a people without peace
Waiting to be saved hopes don't cease

Help us with our last gospel song
Singing of a country to which we belong
With no shame or reference to skin
Just pride for what we've been

The gospel singers with a will to win
A place for the children as equal men and women
Above the threat that black lives don't matter
Accepted as free for the white man to flatter

With respect and equal opportunity
And a future we can see
For we will be what we can be
If America is truly free

I WALKED THE BEACH

I walked the beach with you
And I don't know your name
I held your hand
Until my knuckles were blue

And I don't know why
I called out your name
And it did me no good to try
To remember how I knew it was you

I sat on the bench in the park
And wondered why I was there
Looking for someone to care
And the thought hit me in my ear

That I really had nothing to fear
But the loneliness of selfish thoughts held dear
And my abstract thoughts kept bringing me near
The beach the sunshine the sand

And the tide pounding against my lonely pride
Telling me to think of only one name
Think of only one reason
Think of it until you're the same

As flowers respond to the season
Then we'll know why it's truly us
Nameless timeless but happy in the fraternal tenderness
Lying on the beach

Stretching but reaching for my imagination
It's my spirit why don't I hear it
This sensation that I'm not alone
For there is sand under my feet

And two strides side by side in the tide
Picking me up with my hands tied
Around my heart and I tried
To believe that it was my pride

But it was to my faith I had lied
That God's will isn't aware
Of the doubt and truth I defied
As I walked on the beach of despair

Until it was his hand I held there

ATOM and EVE

It took an atom to make Eve
It took Eve to make Adam
It took formation to make Earth
Who made the atom

Science says it was a blast
Religions say it was a God
Others say it was Mother Nature
Then too it could have been Father Time (travel)

Then there are the creationists
And the sin Satan lists
Intelligent design
Or mine

THE RHOADS THEOREM

The cosmos is the Mather
The white hole is the womb
The black hole is the tomb
And solar energy is the Father

LIFE'S JOURNEY IS NEVER ENDING

Not Darwinian nor Christian
Not the big bang theory
Not Steven Hawking's speculation
But Natural Design

E=MC *squared*
Einstein's theory
Of super time travel
Does unravel… the Rhoads *theorem*

Be it the Earth
The solar system
The stars
The sun and moon

Be it water
Nucleus Neutrons Protons
Molecules
Cells and DNA

All emulating in Adam
And Eve
Solar particles
Called atoms
Be it the sea urchins
Be it under the ground
Or the Queen of the hive
Or human life tis the atom alive

Solar particles are energy
(E=MC2) speed of light squared
Is the spirit and life formed
That has always been
And shall always be

The womb and the tomb that's God
Evolution is the journey
The human spirit is infinity
The story is eternity

Just my opinion – challenge me
But don't criticize the spirit in your eyes
That will see infinity as it never dies
On God's Ship Enterprise

OLD FASHIONED BOY

Tattered and torn
Wearing his Tretorns
In jeans made by Helen of Troy
Just an ole fashioned boy

Humming tunes from the good old days
Hanging moons or exposing a boob
A hold over from the streaker day craze
And water over your head for you tube

We're all just old fashioned boys
Looking good for a weed to buy
Erector sets and tinker toys
Just a steady nice guy

It's a shame with his approach
He'll probably never grow up
Coke cola and 7 Up with a roach
Mixed with bourbon and a cherry in a cup

Just an old fashioned boy once an athlete
Till drugs played games with his mind
And need I repeat
Common sense was buried in his behind

But he's a good ole boy
But around the turn of the full moon
Chasing girls like a clacking pull toy
And the midnight of his last noon

He decided he'd return
Cover up his past and hide his moon
To wait his turn
Just an ole fashioned goon

With an ego to destroy
Until at eighty he'll still be a good ole boy
Needing a compliment turned to joy
Buried under a murky female toy

Trailers on his Harley bike
And his hair flapping in the wind
He ends up just alike
The sad story for many with a fatal end

The bullet tore through his head
Returning him to that simple kid
Just a good ole boy
Who rolled the chamber in that new toy

Just ole fashioned game of Russian roulette
Held it to his head
And said If I'm unlucky with no regret
I'll be dead

Unhappy go lucky as a decoy
Thinking thrills were his only joy
Lived and loved as a good old fashioned boy
Always destined to self-destroy

Dead as the twizzle in his last Rob Roy

GIVE ME MY RIGHTS

I was born on Thanksgiving Day
Baptized on Christmas Day
Raised in a free country somewhat stable
And given the opportunities available

To each sunrise I rose
And as soon as I could stand up and walk
I began chasing whatever I chose
Taking responsibility for what I stalk

And if I play seek and find
I couldn't really blame another
It was I who chose where I signed
Not even my dad or mother

For it was up to me
I really didn't contemplate or tout
That making the most of being free
Is putting my hand out

Or expecting equality from the State
I could stand on my own two feet
Taking care of myself was my family's fate
And the bills I had to meet

Yes freedom to me was an opportunity
But I guess I'm "out of sorts"
Not understanding the system of torts
Nor the courts as a handout of immunity

For they seem to be stating some deed
And protection under the law
About freedoms guaranteed
That kind of hang up in my craw

For Democracy is not a guarantee
Of freedom and equality
It's merely an opportunity for you and me
And those who choose and demand to be free

Though they may lose from their toils
Or are the pathetic hypocrites
Upon which pity spoils
Most likely their lives are the pits

Even though they can climb up on their back legs
With hands out and a lowly soul that begs
I must ignore them for what they are
With their hand in someone else's cookie jar

Barking and begging on their back legs
They're saying I demand equality
I've got the right for my country's free
And we're tis of thee

Though we're supposed to have democracy
Guaranteeing everything to me
So give me my rights to this I demand
And to that to which I stand

Here in this dissolving quick sand
Of patricians under a flag of the red blue and whites
Impairing America's ability to demand
That all living here have to earn their rights

To this Plato understood
Unto which democracy stood
"Where even dogs would want to be free
Standing on their hind legs demanding equality"

And they're never going to be free

MRS. RAPP'S RABBIT TRAP

Just across the alley next door
We've got a neighbor
She ain't no good
Except for chopping wood

And her garden of pride
Growing her favorites outside
Taking her time and resources
To illicit nature's forces

While herself being retired
And a lover of her own life's regard
I guess she got sick and tired
Of her garden being attacked and expired

She sharpened up her hatchet
And her unused hunting knife
She was going to get that hungry rabbit
She'd chase it and grab it's life

Hold it down and stab it
She just had it with that darned ole rabbit
But lo and behold
No matter how hard she tried to get ahold

Of that rabbit
To stab it
She just couldn't catch it
And out of frustration decided
Another way to fetch it

She set herself up a rabbit trap
Yes good old Mrs. Rapp
Cut the grass and sprinkled down some rabbit nap
The trap was set and ready for that rabbit to tap

When no sooner did this Mrs. Rapp
Catch that rabbit in her trap
Then a deathly sly hunter type sap
Tiptoed through the early snow

Disengaged Mrs. Rapp's rabbit trap
Letting that trapped rabbit go
Upon Mrs. Rapp
Return to check on her fie fi foe

Fum not letting Bo Peep's garden grow
Brier Rabbit had ran back into the turnip patch
Only once again avoiding the snatch
Eating and ravaging it's new found catch

So the moral to Mrs. Rapp's Rabbit Trap story
Is the freedom and the glory
Of the rabbit yet able to run
And to nibble lettuce in the sun

While the hunter that let it go
Will someday tiptoe through the early snow
And let the powder of his shot gun go
Hitting his target full blow

Relegating Mrs. Rapp's rabbit to no mo
And to this day the hunter continues
Letting Mrs. Rapp's trapped rabbits go
For his pleasure as hunter's know

Is only the kill not the foe
And of this Mrs. Rapp doesn't even know
She's the perp in this fable
Setting the table for some hunter's table

AN EXTRA MILE

In single file
Can you do it
Can you dig down deep
Till you want to weep
Can you come through it

An extra favor
Can you do it
Can you give before you keep
Even though the price is cheap
And still come through with it

An extra trip
Can you do it
Can you think of others before you leap
Then overcome being called a bleep
And still come through it

An extra smile
Can you do it
Can you take a slap from a red neck
Then stand above it and pick up the check
And come through it

That little extra play
Put forth for the extra mile
Shall put you ahead to stay
And give you an extra happy smile

Just do it I know you are up to it

THE SEA TAKETH

THE SEA TAKETH

The sea takes what it gives
Of the shore
The sea returns to where it lives
Awaiting nature's next down pour

The sea is of us all
Tide pulling at me with its gravity
The sea sounds its call
Wanting my captivity

The sea has me in its grip
It embraces me
The sea is now my ship
To transport me to longevity

The sea is taking me away
On a new journey
The sea for the trip to pray
For peace and tranquility

The sea is for all to retrieve
The spoils of the good earth
Taking what it hath to conceive
Preserving what it's worth

The sea must be free
For us all to conserve
It of waste and debris
And to that we get what we deserve

The sea of being cleansed
By the fronts and pressures
El Nino and La Nina winds
Hiding its treasures

The sea of hurricanes
And its unfriendly calm
Waiting to dash the planes
With its mighty jet stream aplomb

The sea is the only entity
That man cannot tame
With its mighty intensity
Leaving us lame

Only to become tranquil in its place
Misleading us to think
We are in its good grace
Bringing us once again to its brink

The never ending tragedy of the sea's
Gift of the moon tides
Only to taketh the sand away from the day
Making shadows of treasures it hides

In its depth of yesterday

I SAW GOD

I saw God
In our dawn
With his light on
And his love we just found

I saw God
On the beach
With his shells on
And his sand all around

I saw God
In the sea
With his fish tails on
And his tide meeting ground

I saw God
Upon the sky
With his wings on
And his tail windward bound

I saw God
Upon the horizon
With the warmth of the sun
As the day has just begun to resound

I saw God
Twinkling like little lights
From a falling star
That was without a sound

I saw God
In the sunset
With his clouds
Floating shadows on the ground

I saw God
And Jesus at Christmas
As we celebrated
The Kingdom crowned

By the immaculate birth on earth

INTESTINAL AGEITUDE

Intestinal ageitude
The guts to get old
Versus the alternative
An unwish to be old

There's no chains strong enough
To hold doubt
There's no channel deep enough
To drown dread

There's no time like right now
To feel free of doubt and dread by believing that
Age isn't a factor
To the wealth of life

It's great and mean it
This attitude must be
Fostered from an unlikely
Egg of adversity and

It must be emancipated
From a restrictive mind
And planted in the
Heart of a productive believer

Age is merely the past miles
You've covered along the
Shore of opportunity
Getting to the sea of life

So you can partake of its sweetness
Its fragrance its rewards
The sea tis not an age of scars
But a mark of accomplishments

There's no arms strong enough
To prevent fear
There's no scar deep enough
To shed a tear

But any age is strong enough
To enjoy a wife's curves
That endures the family's scars
Healed from fortitude

Inherited as a positive attitude

WON'T BUY MY LOVE

Dollar for dollar
In the US Canada South Africa
Are hanging on to the economies of bluff
But its exchange value won't buy me love

The price is love so give yourself
Pay my price for its right
Shillings can't buy you love
Give me your heart tonight

Francs can't buy me love even as
Rubles fall from above
With Pecos on the wings of a dove
Can't buy me love

Then throw away the Yuan
Don't try to bet on my love for fear
Just give yourself a Lire
To lose my love

Just give yourself a Pound
And take away the Rupee
You will never be able to buy me
Unless the interest will compound

As for the Euro
I have to tell you so
That cash won't flow
If Russia is the foe

And as for the Yen
It would be a sin
To spend down to win
Only to lose out again

Go for the money honey
Can't you see
That the riches are funny
If you want to be debt free

But all I have to offer
Is a romantic affair
Funded by my smile and coffer
Without cash being medium rare

And then if you find someone better
He would have to be a trend setter
Not a bed wetter
With dollars and sense to the letter

$$$$$
BUT $ WON'T BUY MY LOVE
While Lol buys and sells love
On Facebook and my Nook

LIVING BY SUBJECTIVES

What means the most to you
People places or paragons
People shall please you
Places shall appease you
Paragons shall tease you

Objects shall fall
Subjects shall live
Live not by objects
Be not a shallow retainer of things
For things shall crumble to avert
Being dust blown away
On a barren desert

Live by subjects
Be a deep appreciator of people
For only people shall grow
To be the fruit of objects
In a Kingdom of subjects
The King leads for the greater good
In the Kingdom of objects
The King breeds on fear and anger

But the paragon
A model of excellence lives by example
For the subjects and objects are menial
It's a one person show with no second act
Or happy ending
A monarchy is a paragon of that I speak
With the King or Queen as figure heads
And their offspring given lip service for notoriety

Virtues of Democracy and other forms
Of Socioeconomic systems all involve some faith in subjectives
And work for objectives
We believe in a subjective God and hope for an objective life
Meeting our goals and dreams
Above all the graft and schemes

It is a subjective world on an objective planet
Better to be a subject
Than an object
If you could plan it

THE FRIEND SHIP

Friendship is a mighty vessel
On the raging seas of life
As you bob and throb
In the choppy waters once blue
Which want to engulf you

It's good to reach out
And grasp
The lifeline of the friend ship
The mighty ship
As the impulsive wind bounces you about
Pushing you towards doubt

As you're pulled up
Out of the whirlpool
Of reality
Onto the deck of security
You find that real life
Is really very kind
And there's no end
If you've got a windward friend

Who will help you
Set your sail to the wind
And as you shove off
With hopes aloft
Don't forget their name
And do the same

Be the skipper
Of a stable clipper
You'll find that friends are the ship
For every treacherous trip

Ready to equip
The Friend Ship

A SMILE

Light the mouth with love
Light the eyes with devotion
Fill the ears with peaceful sounds
Fill the heart with emotion

To ward off the wolves of tension
To form the sanctity of light's glow
To focus the words to understanding
To open the mind like a fertile meadow

By the five senses of those that sow
As the planter of the seeds
Who will make beautiful flowers grow
Around the weeds

It takes a happy face for a beautiful smile
Frowning makes us visible anger
Warmth brings us near awhile
Coolness pushes us away from danger

Smiling allows me to see your heart
It lights your mouth and eyes with love
It fills your ears and heart with warmth
It is the guiding fingers in my glove

Signifying the emotion of a birth
Of a marriage
Of a peaceful passing
And the creation of a Soul mate

Smile at me and you have me
Nothing could be more true
Than the ring and toasting plea
But you had me at I do

MY SON

My son he said
Dad do you know God
My son I said
Yes he's with us now
Do you know how
Yes my son said
Pointing to his head
Then to his heart
With a smile
He pointed to the sky
Never asking why
He knew
That God is you and I
He's in your head
Through your heart
To your soul
From above
Transformed to love

My son he said
He's in your head
And your bed
After you're wed

WHO CARES

Who cares what time it is
When there is no clock
Who cares what day it is
When there's no calendar
Who cares what year it is
When there is no time like today

I once said
I wish today was dead
And that tomorrow
Was yesterday put to bed
How stupid could I be
To waste away what was given me

Today tomorrow and mystery

Who cares what time it is
When there's no time keeper
Who cares what day it is
When there's no grim reaper
Who cares what year it is
When the mountain only gets steeper

Don't forget to remember tomorrow
The clock's hand knows no sorrow
Who cares who we are
And what I am
Unless I do unless I stand
For the time I have and how I use
My space upon this land

So it's up to me
That I plant and nurture the family tree
The heirs created by me
To make my own destiny

I care what time it is
When there's a legacy
I care what day it is
When my shadow follows me
I care what year it is
When I make work ethically

What else can I say

I live my life for cares
I care what time it is
I care it's all I have today
Tomorrow and yesterday
That's happiness, good health and prosperity

Epitaph Signed by Father Time

EVERY MAN AND WOMAN

Every man and woman must fall
Before they learn to climb
Every man and woman must witness
Before they judge others

Every man and woman must know themselves
Before they can know their work
Every man and woman must lie
Before they can know the effect of truth

Every man and woman must doubt
Before they find the value of faith
Every man and woman must know destruction
Before they can know the feeling of peace

Every man and woman must be hated
Before they appreciate the loss of love
Every man and woman must stand alone
Before they are qualified to lead

Every man and woman must be credible
Before they are capable
To walk in others shoes

To judge themselves for weakness
To know the value of their work
To find faith against all odds
To make peace in midst of war
To appreciate love above those that hate
To lead when there's no followers

When they have to face the facts
With mistakes at their backs
And there is mud in their tracks
With dirt thrown by hacks

It is the strength of their values
To accept failures and setbacks
Which qualify every man and woman we choose
Above all doubt and attacks

In spite of gripes snipes
And peace pipes
Every legendary man and woman
HAVE EARNED THEIR STRIPES

JOEY IS

She's our misty morning
We love her that way
Joey's so sweet beginning
Most any new day

She's our noon day sun
We love that face
Joey's ways mean more fun
So the world is a better place

She's our afternoon delight
We love that smile
Joey's forever racing with all her might
So it is impossible to match her style

She's our evening close
We love those bluish eyes
Joey's look is pure prose
It can quiet her lack of size

She's our everlasting night light
We love her radiance
Joey's spirit is just right
As the sunset plays her dance

She's what gets through the space
That separates day from night
Joey's ways and happy face
Ties us together tight

Kelli Jo is my daughter
We call her Joey for gee whiz
It's her joy and energy fodder
That Joey is

The yellow brick road
The bird in the sky
The ant with a load
The reason we sigh

Kelli Jo on the fly

Running out of her shoes
Faster than a whisper
About good news
After Dan kissed her

When they found out Nate
Was going to occur

THE MIND OF MAN

No man is more than his mind allows him to be
He is born with it for none to see
And once he's of an age to care
It becomes his cross to bear

While the parents influence what's there
Telling and yelling he becomes aware
And from that mind so pure
Comes to some the feeling insecure

For others it's just one constant blur

Because all of us come of age and must take the will
To become more with mortal skill
If we are of a mind to train it well
We'll find a heaven and avoid that hell

With a solitude knowing we can
Being something not an also ran
So you see man's mind is the game
Skin and bones just make the frame

The talent is for the man to tame

If he does it amidst the trials
He'll reap rewards for many miles
Obstacles will come and go
But the mind well trained will know

The good things you reap depend on what we sow
Then on Rushmore they will inscribe
A salute to a mind deft to grow
Not just a man or tribe

The legends thus abide

In Lincoln's chair
Upon Washington's monument
In the unknown soldier's lair
At Kennedy's Camelot to find

All a legacy of Jefferson's mind

A UNIQUE OPPORTUNITY

Every person is unique
Everyone is so slightly different and bold
The eyes the hair the skin the physic
For people don't fit some mold

Amazingly 8 billion individuals
None just alike or the same
For it's the tools and fuels
Giving them the right to be lame

Nor does life limit their fate
To have the freedom to create
To initiate desires
By lighting their fires

To be able to recognize sin's reason
In their own lives to tend
Their plot and plant each season
Then weed their own garden

To be unique
So a unique opportunity
Is one that allows them to seek
Freedom of choice and creativity

Just look at the differences
To appreciate what fate senses
The skin is yellow red or black
Many things that the whites lack

But on the other hand
Is it a tribe flock or band
Organizing the differences
Either for safety or defenses

We become so different
Making our dreams and plans
Our intensions become alike heaven sent
Founded in the same sky and sands

Even in other lands
Our differences aren't fences
Man seems to understand
The reasons for circumstances

For opportunity has no package
Properly addressed to us
Or postage due
On our doubts

We place our bets on chance
That unique opportunity
Risking our bank on Park Place
Waiting for Board Walk's divinity

For Monopoly is real to me

IT'S GONE

A smoke ring will fade
A jet stream will dissipate
My heart is afraid
Our love will have the same fate

Absence should make my need grow fonder
But when you're gone
Long enough to ponder
I'm not sure my image is fond

Because I'm losing my imagination
When I can't see you
And there's no touching sensation
Leaving me cold and blue

Rock cold and getting old
Thought it would never happen to me
I thought we're like gold
Now our love's turning green
Like a tarnished tree

Yes it's gone

The lusty thrill
That makes me shake
Like the bitter chill
After being swept up in anticipation's wake

Nothing better till it's gone
Then we can only remember in awe
About our love's dawn
After it rubbed restraint raw

Covered by the ice of now
As I try to thaw
But don't know how
To bare your only flaw

It just drifted away
In the tide of the past
No more room to play
Once the final stone is cast

It's gone like the clouds of yesterday
Floating along a dark sky
Leaving me without much to say
But so long to your bygone goodbye

THE CAGE

Zoos hold on to their animals
For the sake of humans
Humans cage themselves
To hold off their demons

There are no bars to my cage
There are only scars at my age
Imprisoning me from what I want to do
Can't be free until my sentence is through

My sentence is 40 years in this pittance
Before my fears change the gears
I feel the pressure of settling goals not sure
Looking for my treasure in a sandman's cure

Whether I like it or not
I chose the mold and it's all I got
But before I get too old
I want to kick this cage

Tear down the inhibitions
To my creative age
And pursue my life long ambitions
To write to speak with my play on stage

And to think of more than just the records of the week
Or what other people have in store
I want some freedom to write about good speak
About what is to come through the door

Having been on stage
On this planet of apes
I want out of this cage
So I can squeeze the grapes

The grapes of Wrath
The grapes of Sonoma
The grapes of Rhine
My life an aging of a very good line

Positioned pens are too tight
Novels must grasp the feature
Poetry is too light
No obstacle can confine my censure

I have escaped my gilded cage
By writing my words on this page
To make a day's wage
And settle my caged up rage

And leave the indenture to the zoo

RIDING IN BACK

Riding right here on track
In the back of his Cadillac
Riding in what I lack
Carrying his dreams on my back

Nothing else is so black
As the shining finish of his Cadillac
Just bringing me to his fast track
Then hanging me on his rack

Body built by Fischer Cadillac
Stories told and fantasies unfold
No matter how the cards are stacked
My confidence and goals become bold

But no matter how fast my wheels track
In the driver's seat of my preowned
Cadillac
From Trenton to Hackensack

There's a loser's label in the Livery
Hat and shirt on my back
That puts me in the front seat of his Cadillac
Chauffeur turn here go there ordered from the back

Hey it may not be fair
But it's better than being in the rear
Of someone else's car
Pursuing their career

While my dreams aren't here

It's my choice
It's my voice
I must decide
I run the ride

Whether to be in the black
With my knapsack
Or up front in my used Cadillac
With the wind at my back

Uber livery cabbie fare
All opportunities for employ
May not be there
But it's a ride for pride

Riding in back I would have died

I SAW YOU STANDING THERE

I SAW YOU STANDING THERE

1952

You were in Seventh when I saw you standing there
With your friend with a flair
I was standing there with my stare
Holding my baseball glove my only care

1953

Eight grade wasn't much fun
When all I had was sports in the sun
And I came undone
When you moved to Brooklyn

1954

Ninth grade came along
And when you moved back I still didn't belong
I was too shy and you were wrong
To ignore me in the throng

1955

Tenth grade found us meeting
On the Indianola square
Until I met you with Sam's greeting
Sam and I were an inseparable pair

When I got the courage to ask
We met at The Christmas dance
But we couldn't mask
That it wasn't a true romance

1956

Eleventh grade was the same
Though I was still in the game
After stealing your picture from Sam's billfold
While he slept at my folks house hold

Then lo and behold Sam moved away
But it didn't move me to call Sharon Kay
And to this day she claims
She picked me and took the reins

He returned for the high school prom
Thinking he was her date
And even her mom
Said tell him before it's too late

But the façade took place
So we all could save face
And to this day it's still the case
Of infatuation being our disgrace

To that it's my fancy
Let me say
If it hadn't been for Nancy
Getting us together that Halloween day

(Ten thirty-one nineteen fifty-six
We would never had our wedding anniversary
In the year 2015
Counting up to 56)

1957

Twelfth grade meant time was short
I let Sam feel from afar that she was still his escort
She caught my eye every day at school
But still abiding by the Golden Rule

1958

Heaven and earth came together
When we became one
Not even birds of a feather
Could match our emotion

After her graduation she moved to a new venture
In with her Uncle and Aunt the creature
Breaking us up was hard to do
But we felt we both needed something new

1959

After 180 days apart
Losing our way and my heart
You came back to me
So I could ask and we could marry

2015

I don't think now would be the dream
Of 63 years later the King and Queen
Of sex kids and rock and roll
With each of us giving up our soul

To the Law of Attraction
To our daughters and son
With affection
For the 13 off spring from God above

Keeping us as young as our love

WITHOUT MEANING

Stories without meaning
Mean much to the teller
Mean less to the listener
But may be meaningful

For words are only words
Without a stage a pulpit
Without a page without the players
Speaking their parts

With no meaning
But take the cast on the stage
And read the script each and every
Turning page

From the pulpit
Futures are influenced
By words of life's wit
Spoken for the witnessed

Setting the scene
To every enth detail
Acting out what humanity can mean
Unto others faith must prevail

Actions reactions
Introspection and soulful election
To put it to meaning quotes the absurd
Thought without word

The gestures and illusion's meaning
Can send perception careening
Though different for each listener
Body language means adventure

The act without meaning
Can but emboss an old wine
Unimportant undeniable redeeming
Undefinable travesty of a stale written line

Leaving us with no reason to be so inclined
To learn to earn to spurn to have an inquiring mind
While quiet words spoken in our prayer
Do resonate in the air

 # our viral meaning is still there

WATER TO THE TREE

Who said it couldn't be
Well I've been told
Time after time
That yes goals are fine

But what's going to be will be
No matter what it means to me
I can't buy this and I've proven them wrong
I've proven you can set your sail either short or long

And make it weak or strong unto me
So for those who said it couldn't be
Those imprisoned souls who'll never be free
Let them hear this and reminisce for a fee

About a frog that became a king
A pauper a prince
And a mute who learned to sing
For there is no substitute for common sense

Giving each one the strength to overcome
Doubt fear disability deaf or dumb
The essence of fe fi fo fum
I smell the blood of what I've become

With such will I can grow my creation
Visions and dreams are like water to me
In direct ration to the proportion
Of the water to the tree

Drink me and you will see

SOME PEOPLE

Some people spend their time doubting
Some people spend their time pouting
While some other people are bouting
With little or nothing to gain

Just fighting life in vain
Because you can't beat life
No more than you can stop rain
Or ignore pain

It's a part of the mind's dimension
Emotions and nervous tension
But some people we won't mention
Only stand at attention

Routing themselves towards meaningful goals
Worthwhile and productive souls
And believe me
All people can control the roles

They can be a doubter or an activator
It's their choice
Positive or negative it will occur
Just as much as they speak with their own voice

Some people burn up their energy
They dispel their will
I'm wondering why it's them not me
Deciding the time they kill

And their failure to believe there's a thrill
In setting out a goal
Giving the taker the till
Loving each minute's lull

When they can feel the success in it
Knowing they're not wrong
Or on a streak to quit
No longer weak but strong

Tell me tell me why the fuss
When each and every one of us
Approaches the "Y" in the road
We have to determine our load

While some people spread the seeds
And some only want to reap
As someone else nurtures the weeds
Thinking they're Little Bo Peep

Likely some people are just plain cheap

TELL ME WHY

Tell me why
Birds must die
Yes tell me why
Mice can't fly

Please pray tell me why
I must buy
We have a sky
I just don't know you and why

No more no less
Then the moment
Of your caress
Tell me mortal man
So I can understand

Tell me why
We must die
Why of why
Don't we just fly

Through the clouds
In the sky
Like a bird
Like a forgotten word

Never looking back
For it's a fact
We'll never know why
We'll never feel the clouds in the sky

Perception takes our minds to tell us why
That even mortals may be but a sigh
Because our life is the wink of someone else's eye
Without which we wouldn't live or die

As beauty and truth only exist in the beholder's eye

A REGAL EAGLE

An eagle
A regal a seagull a fighting bull
Who are we
What can we be
When can it be me

No greater than me
I rode the train
Looking for an eagle
Looking for a regal
Looking for pain
To nowhere
Before I found vain
To be the thing you wear

And I got off
My pursuit of the seagull
To find myself some fun
To be the greater than one
That's what I found
That without making a sound
I could apply dreams that fly
Higher than the mortal sky
With the spirit of the fighting bull
And the range of the seagull

By being just me
No eagle can understand
Or make a con man
Nor regal can't stand
Taller and greater
Than a man
Who calls others sir
And is humble
To all
Until he's tall
Riding the train
Beyond being vain

To the heights of God's terrain

BEING LOST

I can think back on times gone by
With a sinking feeling
Of being lost to a helpless try
Monday mornings were blue
And the rest of the week was too

Because the true challenge wasn't there
And I didn't yet know
How much I'd care
About scaling the highest peaks

And weathering the lowest valleys
With a heart that seeks
Dreams among the follies
Being lost I had jobs of drudgery
And I thought myself as inadequate shrubbery

Just decorating someone else's road
And carrying someone else's load
I never really gave it much thought
About the directions that my money bought

I just said yes sir okay boss
I'm secure and the threat of risk is your loss
But I had a shadow will
And my enthusiasm was conspicuously still

Particularly as I became a graduate
And looked for a job
That I thought I might fit
But unfortunately I still hadn't reconciled
A list of goals that I myself had complied

I was doing what I thought I should do
Still fulfilling some else's follow through
Yet really suffering from inadequacy
Feeling always that something was wrong with me

But lo as the table unfolded
And I got bounced around and scolded
Losing my future thought secure
You are fired yes sir

The dawn began to break
And I began to see it was my life at stake
I took a couple of chances
To fulfill some inconspicuous romances

I turned to love
And I found that life wasn't meant to bite
But love her with all my might
My career was meant to love thee
And make you happy

Then it made us aware
That we could right our ship
Totally out of a needs affair
We built a life of a true partnership

With happiness and healthiness as our business

HOLD MY HAND

As I struggle to pursue
Something right something true
I keep looking for you
To give me a route and a clue

Dear God hold my hand
As I stand on the threshold
Of each new adventure
For my legs are unsure

My mind is somewhat insecure
And time flies by in a blur
I think of you daily
Wanting your guidance

To wash away my defiance
Dear God help me walk before I prance
And run before I dance
Dear God hold my hand

If I'm going to lead the band
I must learn to understand principle
Going straight as I make each command
For no peasant shall be my disciple

No jester shall teach that I'm invincible
Lord, give me strength so I can be sensible
When I speak the word upon which we've conferred
To make sense out of the absurd

So absurd is the day that has no direction
If truth melts away
Without purpose in what ones say
And the meanings values decay

In the hands of weak commands
Of the Devil's demands
Dear God hold my hand securely
Walk in my shoes with me

For my last mile to sanity

IT HURTS ME

It hurts me to see you hurt
I just want to die when I see your cry
Yes its way down deep
When I see you weep

It hurts me to see you hurt
It always seems to happen
When the time's not right
Not so much from a disagreement
Or a silly fight

But is hurts most
When I can't touch you and let you know
That I know how you feel
And I love you so

It hurts me to see you hurt
Suffering from senses and feelings
You can't avert
For crying out loud
I can't see you hurt

I keep wondering what I can do
To touch you and help you make it through
And all I can think of
Is to tell you about our love

Hoping my crying will avert
Shallow soothing to your hurt
For if I'm not able to keep you again
I can't live with this nagging pain

It hurts me to be this insane
Though you left me standing in the driving rain
It's Justice for me hurting to restrain
Making you the blame

TALK IS CHEAP

Talk is cheap
If you talk in your sleep
Talk is counting sheep
Tune me in mama tune me in
Tell me I'm talking to a friend
Open your ears mama
Listen to my fears mama
Cause voice is a cheep

When I'm just talking in my sleep
Nothing's real
Nothing that I can feel
Beyond the beating of my own free will
Presuming I have no dreams to kill

Talk is cheap mama
Nod your head mama
And even play dead mama
If you don't know what I mean
Please don't make a scene
Because mama talk is cheap
I can hear you talking in my sleep

Come to me mama
Tell me what you say is true
Tell me it's only me talking to you
Talk is cheap so babble on
Till the crowd is almost gone
Then you can tell me what you mean
Playing out yet another scene
Showing that talk is cheap
So let me go back to sleep

Then it's your lie to keep
Counting countless sheep

IT'S BY DESIGN

We must struggle to be able to be alive
We must believe to be able to conceive
We must live out the design to be able to smile

Our design must be activated
It must be perpetuated
For a teacher it's to follow then lead
For a musician it's to compose
For an artist it's to conceive

THE CONCEPTION

In her fingers curled life
They were so long they covered her face
As she grasped for something to hold
I gave her my hand
She took my finger in hers
And a bond was conceived
And stability a root was set in her mind
That grew through her heart
Crossing with her mother's steady hand
Came a flower to grow its own design
Its own color its own flavor its own inception
The glory of fertile conception

It was a daughter an artisan a babe
A girl a pearl
Kimber Leigh born into our world
By design we uncurl

Her petals her limbs her allure
An artist for sure

BETTER THAN ME

Keeping quiet
Is quite a riot
Since I'm seething with jealousy
Each time you feel better than me

A mother hears her son cry
And we all wonder why
She rushes to his defense
When all he does is whence

A sister hears her brother sigh
And they seem to almost cry
As they blurt out
What siblings are all about

Still a father stands still
Almost crushed by a bitter pill
Having to be made to see
A son should have the right
To feel better than me

So why can't I just smile
And let him know he's not on trial
Why must I look away unhappily
Afraid he'll feel better than me

It must be from childhood
When my parents wouldn't let me feel good
Now that I've understood maybe I'm free
To let my son feel better than me

Setting us apart so his son can be as smart
As he setting him free

EYE OF THE HURRICANE

Down along there between Greenup and Charleston
Five miles from Alsip and big Chalk Taw Run
Stood the Hurricane Baptist Church
The hanging tree and a buzzard on its perch

For it's the message that's blowing in the wind
Which the Good lord meant to send
Catching us all by surprise
Even though it's as natural as the sunrise

Coming on the tail of a vicious storm
Carrying us beyond the norm
Doubting the promise land
For those too few who understand

The essence and the validity of the command
Blowing down that gulley
Blowing up the path
Creating a picture of the other half

For those who take the time
To listen to the chime
And comprehend more than sleeping in the pews
Tithed by reverence as the dues

And though heretics shall search and search
For the singing heard in the chairs
Of the Hurricane Baptist Church
None can really know the answers

Till they hear the wind blow
And understand that there is a Promise Land
And cultivate the seed they sow
Guided by the higher being Ten command

Harken listen-listen please
The sweetest music is blowing through the trees
The driving rain is discipline's pain
But yea it's not all in vain

For in the eye of a hurricane
Shall be peace, love and no one born in vain
Despite black on black crime
Ferguson Chicago Philadelphia

Black lives do matter

THE CHILDREN SAID NO

Life said "come on children
Follow the devil to the sea
Follow temptation set yourself free
Live today and forget yesterday"

Love for tomorrow
Do it their way
Take a drink pop a flight
Get some acid
Get your head out of sight

Don't listen to the skeptics
Come on fly with me
There's no other way
To get so high
That you can't see tragedy

You won't miss what life is about
Feel free to scream and shout
Don't worry about the crash
We'll take good care of you with our cash

Get so numb
Till you're deaf and dumb
Just like a vegetable
Served on my self-destruction's table

Don't take yourself away
Just let it happen
What did you say
You say you don't want to play

While the dealer says no "child don't deny being wild"
What is this nonsense about wanting to pray
And being positive and alert about life style
There's no Karma Darma or a righteous way

You're no fool
You're a product of an educated school
What blight can possibly grow
A Satan when the children say no

When the children emphatically and absolutely
Say no to drugs, alcohol and cigarettes
Their chance at love hope and romance
Will take them as far aa they want to dance
No way will I destroy today
For the promise of only getting away
From myself only to delay
My future stoned away

Beheaded by meth
Imprisoned by the white horse
Black lungs by grass
Cocaine in the brain
And crack cocktails stuck up your…

Children oh so innocent
Say no to self-decent

THE SPRINGTIME OF OUR LIVES

The spring of our lives
Is the spring of our certainty
And the beginning that thrives
On it's the encore to matrimony

Our symphony will play forever
As we stand here holding hands
In the springtime of love's favor
To be sealed by wedding bands

The minister begins to speak
Knowing it was something we seek
Not realizing why the birds had words
And the bees could sing

Louder than each other in spring
And the warmth of the day
Must have had something
To make them hover that way

All around us just above
Our springtime love
Senses were flying too
As my lips touched you

Warming our bodies through and through
Like the springtime embrace
Of the sun rising to blue
Smiles and shadows spread a caress

Upon what the past had said
And to this we'll always be wed
By the springtime memories
Running from those petals we fled

To our car made up with words to digest
With me splitting out of my vest
And your dress a mess
From that corsage pinned to your chest

Off we went to a honey moon in our best
A motel then a hotel then a cruise to be assessed
With our desire and love we caressed
Having the time of our lives we are blessed

As summer and fall of our lives set in
We had children
Who then had their children
Who will have their children
As we pray that there will be no end

Now in November it's 56 years later
Our wedding anniversary and the winter sets in
Each year we thank our creator
For where we are going and where we've been

Always the springtime of our lives with my best friend

SANDMAN

What did you say Sandman
What do you say to a dreamer
You say it won't bury me in the sand
But naiveté can hurt a schemer

I could tell by the way you said sir
And not what you said
Open to the last chapter
By looking at your page I've read

"The Golden rule rules
Those with the Gold rule
I learned that in MBA school"

To the point but somewhat blunt
In the end the elf becomes a tyrant
Who pulled one too many stunts
Where giants turn to runts

I said to the seed who became a beanstalk

"Actions speak louder than words
And sour turns to curds
Because if left to its devices
Reality is concealed by disguise and vices

"But if you taste it enough times
Even good intentions are crimes
If they don't abide
Coincide and take pride"

"In the laws of the land
And to those who yet don't understand
All mortals live by the same command
To be the leader of the band"

"Live a life of sin
And you'll never win
Live a life of good
And you'll end up where you should"
Then the Giant said falling on his head

"Poppy cock
The Golden rule rules
Those with the Gold rule
I learned that in MBA school"

"What did you say sir
What did you say to get ahead
I guess I misunderstood you
When you said its where your butter is bred"

"Because if what you say is true
I read just the opposite in you
Just looking at your behavior
Tells me we're through"

"And you're left
With your own sand to chew"

STONED SOBER

STONED SOBER

Stoned to death by an enemy
Stoned by a dummy with a needle
Stoned to nothing by a lover
Stoned to something by a magazine cover

Getting high on living is one thing
Getting high on dying is the final fling
Getting high on the wire to death
Is like getting scared when you run out of breath

Life is so short and abrupt
When it's too fast and corrupt
But as we age
We start looking at the last page

Because growing up is so hard to do
But growing old is harder too
When there's nothing to hang onto
Be it a love a family a dollar bill or a last will

Hanging on is so hard to do

Sounds too good to be true
That living is for dying
And loving someone like you
Is really getting high on trying

Like touching your toes
With your fingers then your nose
Stretching yourself beyond your shoes
And never singing the blues

Getting high on buying flowers
For the weekend not just wedding showers
Giving her your time and attention
Without breeding lovesick tension

Famous last rites for the addict

RIP "Once I got stoned on the smell of grass
I thought I was walking on water in the rain
When I sobered up all I did was smash
My head into the wall of pain"

Then I got stoned sober

I got stoned sober on you there
You with your beautiful charm and sexy body
People said I looked like I was walking on air
And I didn't even need that chemical toddy

Stoned sober in my heart if we ever part

HOLD ME TILL I CRY

Tears are no cure for loneliness
Hanging on can make you sad
But I'm compelled to love your kiss
Even though I think you're GLAD

For me for you
Something old and something new
Hold me till I turn blue
Look me in the eye
Ask me simply why

Why when you hold me
Do I begin to cry
Laughter is no proof of happiness
Nor is the feeling of a caress

Just enough to discourage me
Because I know you're real
You I can touch and know you feel
For the private moments we steal

While money or wealth is no cure
For our need to be secure
Nor is good fortune necessarily impure
When my good fortune is yours

And though it's nothing brand new
I want to cry when I hold you
I want to fly when you mold me
I want to die when you scold me

Then if we were to part
Don't take advantage of this gentle heart
Because I know I can never cry again
If you decide not to remain

In the custody of our married name

HAPPINESS IS

Reaching the destination of a long trip
As your children are losing their grip

Happiness is an enthusiastic compliment
By someone you thought you should resent

Happiness is the embrace of a friend
With whom you would face the end

Happiness is the pride you take in a child
Converted to being calm not wild

Happiness is the softness of your homeward bed
And the dawning of a day you don't dread

Happiness is the smiling face of your love
When she finds out its her you're thinking of

Happiness is plotting out your erstwhile course
And the feeling you've been touched by the force

Happiness is nine years of effort
That to a success you can convert

Happiness is a thought of yesterday with a smile
And a look to tomorrow as a worthwhile mile

Happiness is not being unhappy with yourself
But be content to up the time invested in your health

Happiness is a trip with interesting parking places
And a mind that is filling those spaces with aces

Happiness is the smell of a new car or house
And the contentment expressed by your spouse

Happiness is the ability to say gee whiz
I gave to the cause because it's his

Happiness is eat drink and merriment
And feeling your purpose is well meant

Happiness is the meaning of a good poem sung as a song
And the fulfillment of wanting to belong

Happiness is perfecting your ground stroke
With the feeling you can go for broke

Shoot the moon roll the dice

Knowing final happiness
Is in the hands of Christ

With the urge to win
Is of mice and men

WHAT WOULD YOU DO

What would you do
If this were your last day
The finale to you
What are you going to brew

Would you sit back
And regret that it's done
Or remember those victories
You might have won

My friend this is the question
Using a bucket list to send
How to use today if it were the end
That's in blowing in the wind

I'm afraid
If you would say
Give me passed records to play
Or pray for another day

You'd regret the final sunset
And lose your last bet
And fail to seek so you will find
That last day would be kind

With joy not confined
To worry or folly of the mind
Worrying about the end
Or fences you had to mend

By just smelling each flower
You could be happy singing in the shower
And breathing the surf
Living for all its worth

To have one more day
And have no regrets
When that day's sun sets
You'd be all in with your bets

That to reap the harvest you must sow
Happiness before you go

THE TEN COMMANMENTS OF LOVE

Burning Bush
Sermon on the Mount
The Lord's Prayer
The Ten Commandments of life

Etched in the minds of lovers
Called Love that the Messiah said

#1 Thou shalt not love another as you love me now

#2 Thou shalt not be true to another until to yourself you are true

#3 Thou shalt not lie nor gamble for love

#4 Thou shalt not love if it's for yourself alone

#5 Thou shalt not give of yourself without love as the reason

#6 Thou shalt not make a seed from yourself and abort procreation

#7 Thou shalt not squander love for money

#8 Thou shalt not covet your neighbor's wife

#9 Thou shalt not reject your lover's bed

#10 Thou shalt not leave the family to another

These are the commandments I leave with you
Take of them hold them true
For Heaven awaits
True lovers' fates

ETERNITY

Arabic interpretation

The story has it that once every two thousand years
A white dove flies over the Sahara
And plucks one grain of sand from the desert
When the dove has removed all of the sand grains
From the Sahara leaving it bare eternity begins

Poet's interpretation

Eternity settles over the Sahara
The sands await the white dove
For it appears each second millennium
Dropping to the timeless love
It has for each grain
Taken to its resting place
Among another times terrain

This is but the start of the endless hourglass
That the mortal fears
Each grain plucked from the infinite
By a trip every two thousand years
Faithfully the bearer returns with the wind
To mark the time upon the scroll
Of a history that will never end

Eternity then is forever and because of life there is a blend
Only if we think beyond ourselves
To that we're asked to comprehend
For as the dove marks the moons one grain at a time
Until the desert lies barren of its dunes
Then and only then does Eternity begin
As reality swoons

And without the dove and love
There's no realty but the moons

NUMBER ONE

Enthusiasm is the fuel
For a hungry mind
Attitude of mind is the motor
That generates enthusiasm

One feeds upon the other
Until they become number one
This designation is for the soul

Character desire and determination
Rolled into the number one goal
Is the heart

To be number one with oneself
Requires discipline
To do so the will to envision is the act

The act to do so doesn't just happen
It comes about because of faith
To take a risk with effort

Knowing effort will pay off in multiples
For those who are adept
Shall act upon a persistence to attain success

They shall overcome obstacles
For the sake of the ingredients and tenacity
To be number one

A *ttitude*

D *iscipline*

E *ffort*

P *ersistence*

T *enacity*

Adept not for themselves but for fulfillment
Through moving others to be their own number one

FOR THE PERSISTENT

Desire is in the blood of a dreamer
Aspiration is in the vision of a conceiver
Good sense is in the head of a leader
Strength is in the shoulders of a go getter

Love is in the heart of the giver
Faith is in the soul of a believer
Steadiness is in the step of an achiever
Firmness is in the hands of a helper

Confidence is in the smile of a healer
Softness is in the eyes of the lover
Inquiry is in the mind of the teacher
Sharing is in the gifts of the mother
Competing is in the strength of the father

FOR THE INSISTENT

Doubting is in the tears of the pouter
Denying is in the face of the liar
Rejecting is in the words of the buyer
Losing is in the eyes of the doubter
Fearing is in the life of the mentor
Swearing is in the mouth of the actor

Being suitors of either negative or positive results

All are portraying their personalities at their best
Which aren't interchangeable with their words
To know the truth just look listen and assess
What they do afterwards

For persistence can't overcome common sense

PEOPLE ARE PEOPLE

Houdini was a magician
A purveyor of illusion
Hitler was a maniac
A servant to none
Mother Teresa was an angel
A servant to many
Muhammed was a prophet
A servant of peace

Who are you
Why are you you
Answers are few
Questions are many

About your humanity

Jackie Robinson was a role model
Martin Luther King was a change agent
President Truman was a pragmatist
To Jo was a masochist

What are you
How are you
Answers are few
Questions are many

For your posterity

Your mother was love
Your father was spirit
Your children are your heart
Your grandchildren your soul

Is that you
Do you feel it
Answers are few
Questions are many

For your sincerity

People are people
Do what you do
But no matter what
Please get caught… Just being you

DIFFERENT

Different we are
All the product of our star
Wasting away in some bar
Or perishing in our car

Since we're all different
Are we heaven sent
Or just here for rent
A body in decent

Born to please
Here to squeeze
Left flapping in the breeze
Like some unhealthy sneeze

Some are for beauty
Some are for duty
Or making it as a cutey
With a rack and booty

Eight billion of us
On this earthly bus
Full of vigor and fuss
Going somewhere or bust

Running into each other
Even our sister or brother
Loving each and another
Or the same if you druther

Living it up and living it down
Be us a jester or the clown
All feel we are heaven bound
Until Hell brings us down

All for anticipating the end
When we will need a friend
Or one more day for rent
As our body does relent

Finding that our spirit truly is Heaven sent

THE MIND GARDENER

The gardener of a self
What a beautiful thing
Planted in the garden of opportunity
Cultivated by the souls with a purpose

To improve themselves
And the garden around them
This garden of opportunity
Is God's laboratory
For future's story

He planted the seed of knowledge
In the selves that
Dwell in the garden of opportunity
Some will waste their fertility
Some will experiment and question
Their garden's virility

Wanting to know why
They live out their time
And waste their opportunity
Others will take pride in the harvest
By watching a fertile dream grow
Into virtual realty

Realizing that success
Unlimited awaits those
Who understand celebrity
That decorates history's puberty

For the garden of opportunity
Is the very shore of destiny
Syphoned through the sand
By a bird in the hand

A SET BACK

If you get off track
You've likely been set back
With the fits and scorn

May make you forlorn

But it's up to you to be reborn
Get back on your toes
Only a healthy root grows

Failure is a state of mind
Putting you on your heels
Or on your back

I don't care
If it's hard luck
Or what you lack

Just fight your fight
And smite the fright
Turn your reverse gear around

Until the forward gear is found

Anyone can get down
Only a few though
Know it's true

That a comeback is made by you

The tracks are laid
In the mortar of a set back
Three steps back two steps forward

That's progress that's success
That can be happiness
By learning to walk forward

Not stepping behind a set back

END OF BEGINNINGS

Why are we sitting
Here touching the
End of new beginnings
When we're together wanton
For past beginnings
That will not be forgotten

Or are we circling back
To ourselves
In another time and place
A different body and face
Reincarnated from inner space
Leaving loose ends without a trace

Will this mean there is no God
Just an emesis bowl
And a flow of atoms into cells
Colliding into each other's time
Creating a mass of proteins and neurons

Named in the honor of humanity
Or in the image of a true God
That also plants the seeds of nature
And the creatures under his sun
On the Good Ship Earth

For taking these beginning gs to an end
Of doubts and fears of deçlining years
Looking to the rebirth
Of the beginning
Of a mortal universe without end

Called death of body and rebirth of men

REPLAY ME

Like a record that's heard
With a tune that's new
My feeling is a word
Said just to you

The word is love
Played by angels from where ever
On my heart
Strung together not apart

Like a haunting tune
Replay me with the moon
Recounting for never
Returning as the groom

Replay me
Regain me
Reward me
With your love

A pitch on key

Words sung low
Sweet music to bestow
Feelings from the soul
For your mate's toll

Replaying forever
My words to you
Loving words in my quiver
Shot to the tune so true

Into your heart
While cupid stands by
Playing his harp
Making you cry

As instant replay sings "our love will never die"

PURITY

Conceived in purity
As a newborn child
Loved and cuddled
A blessing to be befuddled

Pushed and shoved
Not always loved
Do we realize
This child
We can't civilize

Conceived in purity
Left to scar
Like the falling
Of an unknown star

There will be few
As this story comes true
That retain
That innocent refrain

For life blots out
What reality can be
A purest heart
Delivered upon Society

Conceived in purity
Close but not that far
Between those we lose
And those we scar

Each is each
To his or her own
Some together
Some alone

Life is a pure gamble with
No rhyme or reason to his and her
Together it does occur
That there is no reason… to be alone

Only the lonely don't want to go back home

ALIBIS

Looking through blinded eyes
Making time with
Mindless lies

Hearing through deafened ears
Blotting out
Senseless tears

Feeling through a cold heart
Stopping love as a
Careless reason for being apart

Speaking through an immoral voice
Asking to be God's
Only choice

Looking with no eyes
Hearing with no ears
Feeling with no heart
Speaking with no voice
Making mindless lies and alibis

That's the life of a liar
For himself he's on fire
Penance belies the alibis
If self-preservation is dire

Making excuses
For physical abuses
Of life and limb
Hurting upon a whim

All characteristics of alibis
Right before our eyes
The abuser lies
Then the reason dies

Whether sexual
Physical or mental
Abuse is real
And it will destroy those that feel

Repenting is not enough
Calling the abuser's bluff
Isn't about hate or show and tell
Or is the patient well

Making alibis to the Devil
Is the deepest well
And the hottest spell
Once you've abused and fell

It's about redemption in Hell

MY SHADOW

MY SHADOW

Look and ye shall find
Your spirit close behind
Sneaking in and about
If the lights gone out

Like the soul is hidden
Beneath the skin
Shy and forbidden
Hidden the souls of men

Could it be
Lurking just behind
My spirit follows me
A figment of my mind

Called my shadow
Quiet does it cling
Or come and go
Like a kite on a string

It's a miracle
A thing to behold
With no obstacle
It can't be controlled

So free
So unreal
Always a part of me
But no touch to feel

Look and you will see
As it catches up and falls behind me
That it can be a part of you to find
The shadows in your mind

Speed it up
Slow it down
Pour it from your cup
It has no sound

It's like your spirit
Only floating away
If you decide to quit
Or forget to pray

Don't step on it
As it comes along
Ignored and unfit
Trying to belong

Though it can't hide
You can pull it in
By going inside
To where it's been

Away from the light
Into the dark
No longer in flight
It can't embark

Though some say
It's up to the sun
To create it each day
The shadow is never done

It is a touch of creation
Like the cloudy sky
Into the human station
Living in the dark too tired to fly

Until unleashed by the mighty sun
Darkness ending and the shadow just begun
Can't be caught can't be bought
If you turn it out
You will be an ink spot

THE ME SOCIETY

You caught me looking at you
Looking at him
Looking at me

It's a mixed up society
Couples no longer are necessary
When the me's decide to triple up

And the different sexes
Become lovers and mixes
Avoiding the labels and fixes

In the old days
Queers and fags were outcasts
Now it only as long as it lasts

Not to be judgmental
But the me society
Isn't looking for free

They want to be accepted
And they are just like me
Not wanting to be tested or bested

Now I see you're looking at me
Looking at me in the window
For something free

I look back and lo and behold
You're smiling at Jack
Who is off his game with a dame

He then looks at me looking at you
And gives me the thumbs up
For the way you are now looking at me

Togetherness how nice
With fun and without vice
Not having the pay or quote a price

The only suits we pay for
Are hanging in Macey's and
Don't include the other 'tutes

Prostitutes aren't looking at you
Looking at me looking to do it for free
It's still a me society

DESTINY

Destiny is as deep as the darkest cave
Destiny is as vast as the genius mind
Destiny is as exciting as the newborn baby cry
Destiny is yours only if you try

The deepest cave has no light
Until a human enters

The human mind is not bright
Until learning sets in

The newborn cry doesn't start
Until the human hand is put in motion

Trying consists of the human mind
And hand guided by emotion

Possibly you are destined for greater things
Possibly you will map your own destiny
Possibly you will act and do it right
Possibility sets in with actions committed
Only if you might

Push your apprehensions away
Incriminate the natural sinners
Pull up your confidence
Believe in the right until each day's end
Surround yourself with winners
The way is this my friend

Destiny isn't awaiting the estranged
Practice this even though others see it as funny
Don't accept that it can't be changed
Don't lay the principle down for the sake of money

MOTHER NATURE

Mother Nature is on my mind
She dominates the spaces
That my work can't find

Mother Nature is oh so much
When we work together
Time stops to our touch

Mother Nature we held off so long
Then for a reason only you control
We began our love song

Mother Nature we need each other
As a poem needs heard
As sister needs brother

Mother Nature why aren't we just
The chances are who knows
We may be doing what we chose

Mother Nature it's truly a wonder
Let's take the chance on what to do
I can't bear for doubt to do us under

Mother Nature when I lie here in my grave
I feel your magic
Surging from my soul that you save

Mother Nature as silence is your music
Let your magic be my command
It is that feeling I seek

As a Renaissance man

Mother Nature is a common personification of natural resources that focuses on the life-giving and nurturing aspects of life by embodying it, in the context of a super natural mother

WITNESS

As you are my witness
Why don't you speak up
Do you fear the truth
Don't you know to do otherwise is corrupt

All I'm asking is that you remember
To the best of your charity
What really happened
When they crucified me

Because you see
I have come back
I'm not buried forever in the pack
Because I've got what my enemies lack

That's faith in the truth
Upheld at any cost
Attempting to avoid the smallest sooth
Even if life be lost

Now that I need you where are you
You've always said I was your friend
We've faced many mountains us two
I hope this isn't the end

But if you don't show me you're not afraid
And that you have faith In destiny
Remember that bed you've made
With a character that's in jeopardy

It's your decision to make
It's really not do or die
It's just your principles you forsake
And sever our bonded tie

I've never lied for you
And I'm not asking you to lie for me
For what I ask is true
Just help me show it for all to see

You are my witness
You are my hope
And I understand your stress
But you must have the will to cope

Stand up then and with your voice
Don't be afraid to speak
Your character is being tested you have no choice
To scale or fail life's most meaningful peak

You say you can't do it
You say the risk is too high
You say you can't sit
With me if it's do or die

Yes… yes I understand
It's really every man's trade
For security that turns to sand
When you're tested and you become afraid

I hope you learn a lesson from this
I must go now
To find a witness that won't dismiss
That truth abides somehow

They're not everywhere
But truth will endow
Fetching them here
To take the oath and vow

To bear witness by supporting facts somehow

DESOLATE OR VIBRANT

Standing in the foreground are the remnants
Of ages gone by
That train that trekked into the sun
No longer lines the sky

There too were phones that hung on the lines
Which are gone to stay
Now news seeking an ear must pass
By some other way

A cell phone is now a camera
Texting is being alone together
Selfie's are quick incrimination
Snap is avoiding permanence

Notice that the past is not the theme
Forsaken for its cast while… solitude
Finds peace in another day
And takes the highway another mile

The fields are shadows outlining the crops
Beneath a falling summer sun
Waiting for a car or wind to break
A sound for silence done

Loneliness is for you the traveler
Coming on this scene
Sadden by no way in which to carve
Meaning into this screen

Harken though more is certainly there
To mark the lifeless terrain
Pulsating are the rays as they emanate
From a vibrant spiritual refrain

The poet's prayer
Help me
My thoughts are always seeking
Out a meaning true
Please direct through the haze
Lest my world's askew

The mind must be vibrant not desolate

Desolate… devoid of inhabitants… vibrant… pulsating with life

THE PAUPER'S LEDGER

Who's on first
Who's ahead
What's success
To hell with Spieth who's who
I say

It matters not super star
Who you are
Or what you claim
Just what you aim

It matters more
What you are
And at whose door
Kneels an aspiring super star

The differences between
Those that do
And those that don't become a king or queen
Are mighty but so few

They're hidden in a pauper's ledger
If we look and find
Kindness
Persistence
Spirit
Humility
Commitment
Sincerity

Even so the most important difference that will
Give your Ledger wealth and prosperity… is skill

William Tell
Alexander Bell
Dolly Parton
Dean Martin

Or is it a mother's children who dwell in hell
Is it a sports hero who excel
Is it a Politian who can't spell
Or is it the handy man who
Speaks three languages well

They are All-Americans until they fail
Even then they're better than snail mail

TAINTED GLASS

Taint the glass
Make it glow
Will it pass
Will it blow

Into a work of art
Making beautiful fixtures
That stand apart
From ordinary creatures

Like sunshine upon the window
Showing life oh so clear
No pretense though
Shadows may appear

If it darkens as it must
Paint the glass with color
Brighten the view it's just
To clear his vision with vigor

Feelings for those with hope
Forsaking the sun for self
Losing the battle of will to cope
Color them a black life without health

Piety uses a painted glass
For its reverent purpose
To covet a mortal class
Creating a positive surface

Bringing smiles is alright
Feeling good almost quaint
Let in the light
Be it sunshine or paint

For sun or painted candor
Warms us with this vision
Set up free of slander
And shadows without treason

This is the halo he wears
Window shows me
With hopeful treasures
Brightness for all to see

Saving lives from tainted pleasures

EMPTY ARMS

I lay here in your arms
After we're through
And I know
There's no one but you

But when we're up
And we go our way
Doubts corrupt
As life gets in the way

If we want what might have been
Others come by
In spite of their sin
They make us cry

With empty arms
I'm back to needing you
With open arms I'm back it's true
For your body's charms

But then life gets in the way
We feel we're not the same
Fighting the doubt to stay
When I'm really to blame

Keep me
Lay me down
Hush my mouth
Make no sound

Turn my ego to charms
Pull me to your skin
Kiss me hold me
In your longing arms

Once I'm there keep me
Fold me in your grasp
Hold me in your empty arms I plea
And you'll see at last

How life can get in the way

STAIN ON MY PILLOW

Wake up you fool
Your mind is just on a trip
Pull back to reality
Before the scales are tipped

When you cry in your sleep
Towards the aura of insomnia
Is it apnea or counting sheep
That holds back the urge of mania

Look at it like the weeping willow
In a dreamer's state
So what if tears stain the pillow
Fever isn't until you awake

Shedding your mind of stress
And rid your brain of fear
Doesn't come by getting undressed
Or sweet dreams my dear

Dreaming it seems comes on
Around the turn of dawn
When your mate is gone
And you're the lone one

Then daylight stability rises
With the sun
So my head is full of surprises
Confidence gone before the day is done

Hanging my head like a weeping willow
Dreams never really happen anyway
The stain is still on the pillow
And my thoughts willow away

Circumstances seem to stain
My pillow when my love is in vain
When clouds turn to rain
And my heart is in pain

Either I get a new pillow or change where I'm lain

NOT TOO OLD TO LOVE

Love they say is for the very young
That's how stories are told and songs are sung
If this is true
What youngster is loving you

Cause as the story goes
Only young love grows and grows
Tis a lie I reply
Proven as my tears won't dry

Most certainly infatuation isn't love
It's only the feathers on the turtle dove
The longer it exists the more it persists
Like the desire of a youngster's first kiss

For no one is too old to need
As all hearts will surly bleed
For another human being
Held for the feeling and seeing

Surely love is for all ages
Though it comes in stages
And the passion careens
So long as we have romantic genes

I'm finding that true love is ageless
As shown by the female caress
From ourselves to our mothers
And even when we're not soul brothers

Love they say is for the youngster
So I guess I'm a frustrated spinster
Who is bold and hoping is my thing
Until there is a proposal and a ring

Got to find me that one before my time is done

GIVE TO GET

We live we die
In between we give

We talk we cry
In between we try

We love we feel
In between we keel

We work we labor
In between ours and our neighbor

We study we learn
In between is our concern

We receive we send
In between is our friend

We lust we must
In between we trust

We burn we yearn
In between we discern

Whether to give
To receive
For to live isn't
To deceive
One's self
One's neighbor
One's friend

One's God
Who gave his only son
To receive the faithful flock
To God's will be done

Give some and get Kingdom come

NOVENNA

Nova the Mother was a lovely star
Urus the sun god was the Father
They came together in love
To conceive Novenna

She was the birthright of the heavens
Her brilliance was of tomorrow
Her beauty of today
Her journey is from yesterday

Novenna the ballerina of the skies
Smiling down upon us though poor
She's the sign of what angel's do apprise
Leading us past the days of yore

If you're wise to follow
Novenna is reality
A hand held out to you
Grasp her to lead you through

The offspring of Novenna
For she wed the North Star
The brightest star of all
Mated they gave birth

To the universe
Their family of nine
Were very special
They were set in time

A family facing a black hole
Its widow maker out in space
luring these nine planets whole
One became the white hole's mace

Called Earth by Novenna
It thrived like no other
Young Star
The Father he did its surface
The Mother touched its skin
It took on its Mother's beauty
And the Father's light
It has been many years now
As Novenna became the

Very Mother Nature
Of Earth's existence
Unto this came the miracle
Of another being

Conceived by Earth's Father's warmth
And Novenna fertility
Lo Earth had given life
To you and me

Blessing us with our Mother's Nature
As our Father's fertile rays
Created us as men and women on Earth
Us the mortal men and women

Are here but for a while
For Novenna and our Father
Have eternity to beguile
As their children we are of them

And into them we will pass
Pass into the very existence
Into the gentle hands
Of Novenna

Of our Mother's Nature
Of our Father who art in Heaven
Our resting place
As one of the nine offspring in space

Mercury the warmest
Venus the most beautiful
Earth the living nature
Mars the red dust
Jupiter the giant of gaseous clouds
Saturn the colorful gas rings
Uranus the ice giant
Neptune the bluest seas
Pluto the farthest step child

And their offspring
Ceres the dwarf star
Haumea the asteroid

Make... make the comet
Eris the beta particle
Orcus the dark matter
Quaoar the alpha particle
2007 O10 the atom
Sedna the neutron
The White Hole the womb
The Black Hole the tomb

Under the God Father Sun
And the God Mother Moon
All lives matter

DON'T WALK ON MY GRAVE

DON'T WALK ON MY GRAVE

They actually gunned me down
The duel was for real
Their bullets were a biting round
And got me good before I had a chance to keel

They even dug my grave before I died
Expecting me to fall in
Hoping I would fall before I cried
And sacrificing my chance to confess sin

As if time had come they spate the eulogy
"Here we lay this child
For dreams he couldn't flee
And ideals thought too wild"

They closed the lid so now it's dark
As my world falls in
Leaving only righteous signs to mark
My way out from this gory end

As their footsteps disappeared
In the soft earth above my head
They walked on my gave nothing feared
Mincing principles they thought dead

But I put on my cape to escape turning to dust
With many lessons learned
By keeping my head and spirit in trust
I skirted their sentry left unconcerned

And despite my disciples who were singing
"Walk on his shadow knave
Walk on his image
Walk on his senses
But don't walk on his grave"

The gravediggers then dug their own grave
Singing
"Don't walk on any man's grave
Because what he stood for and gave
Will haunt you so be aware
You're next to be there"

"Praise be the spirit of he
Who died and rose in
His own image as his Judas
Cried out "he must die for sin"

Epitaph at my funeral
So I did confess my shallow pride
Serving those that to themselves have lied
No life is in vain if life is eternal

Leaving some to heaven and others to the inferno

SAVE ME

I ain't got no money
Ain't got no friends
Ain't got no hope
Save me for ain't isn't me

This is the way of people
This is the way they stand before the steeple
Asking for help
With a selfish yelp

They don't take time
To look inside
They just whine
Till they've died

My lord
What a waste
It's a two edged sword
If the self were faced

How then
Can these people be saved
By the commandments ten
If they haven't behaved

The only way to bring it to you
Is to think it through
Until you know it's you
That must be true

Saved if that's
What you've craved
Let it be
Only after you see
That the savior is thee

And saving isn't free

AGING FACES

Faces they are a changing
As our body rearranges
From the process of aging
Pictures on yellowing pages

It's the same ole story
As the world turns
The hands of time
And we can't stand still
Through the ages

Faces they're a changing
For each second comes a wrinkle
For each minute a stoop
For each hour a gray temple
Through the ages

Since the parents
Put the clocks in motion
Faces in the crowd
They're a changing
Through the ages

It's the same ole story
As the world turns
And we can't stand still
To the motion of time
A second
A minute
An hour
Through the ages

Passing is the last shower
The wake
The funeral
Of another day
Through the ages

It's the same ole story
As the world turns
And we can't stand still
To the motion of time
The tread mill
The walking track
The climbing wall
Keeps us fit and well
Through the ages

And the ages fill
Our veins with rifts
Our will with shifts
Our skill with miffs
Our hope with gifts
Our faces with lifts
All with God's good graces

Faces they're a changing
For each second comes a wrinkle
For each minute a stoop
For each hour a gray temple
For each day we grapple
For each year like Adam's apple
We look for Eve's dimple

SHEBA

Sheba's a cat
Sheba's mine no Clementine
When I hold her
And I unfold her
I soon find
Sheba's heart is unkind

Sheba's mystery is
Sheba's history was
Sheba's no Clementine

Sheba's rare
Sheba's soul is bare
Too bad Sheba doesn't care

Sheba's between each line
Of my poetic rhyme
To bad Sheba's eyes are blind

She's divine
Sheba's fine
Too bad Sheba doesn't mind

Sheba's mine
Sheba's every time
But you can't hold her

Nor scold her
Maybe we'll find
Sheba's heart there untwined

In her catnap
Or Her feline
Fury behind

Sheba's mystery is
Sheba's history was
Sheba's no Clementine

Sheba was afraid
That when we moved
She strayed and stayed

Broke our hearts
Hoping she's not dead
We never could replace her instead

Why she was fine
Most of the time
But she was no Clementine

MAN GRAVE

Marking the passing
This way
And where the bodies lay
Headstones like souls
Don't decay
Unless they're lost
On Memorial Day

So mortals
Make your mark
Shed the light
Upon the dark
Don't let your soul
Delay
On Judgment Day

Select your headstone
As you pray
For an epitaph
Passing this way
Selected now
As you live
Receiving less than
You give

Putting the words
To stone
And never be alone
No sins to atone
Yes read the mark
It's a hard day's night
In Jurassic Park

For the grim reaper
When funerals are cheaper
Tombstones for Sale
Brimstones from Hell

CRYSTAL BALL

CRYSTAL BALL

(The BIBLE)

Look and ye shall find
Harken to the sign
Raise the shade
And pull the blinds
Open the future
Look between your life lines

Is it more than you can dare
Is destiny really there
Only to those aware

Look into my crystal Bible
God said
To fate we thee wed
From the cradle to the bed
Unto a spirit once thought dead

So believe you can
So believe that in time
Sketched on your hand
Is within your price line

The answer's there
Listen to the wind bow
The spirits call
As mortals weep
To the crystal ball
Before you do sleep

When you hear without fear
Then you will know
What makes the ill wind blow
Through the crystal ball
As God watches us fall

Then tells Jesus on us all
With our life line
And our horoscope sign
So the stars align

In a heaven on earth we must find

LIFE AS AN ICICLE

What do you see
What do you feel
When you find a trickle
Growing into an icicle
Reflecting the sun
Catching the light
Sparking fun
With the colors bright

What do you see
What do you feel
When you look through
A banana peel
A piece of steel
A Willow tree
A raging sea
I see a life
I see chemistry
Like the edge of a knife
Cutting away the mystery

What do you see
What do you feel
When you find a trickle
Growing into an icicle
The mystery of nature
Flowing into an ice sculpture
Forming each creature
Under the creator's sun
And someday to that end
It will melt
Returning to the sun
As a solar particle of beauty

LISTEN TO THE WORLD TURN

Once the world
Was thought Flat
And turning backwards
To be exact

Then it was Aristotle
Speculating that it was round
With Europe on top
And America upside down

Then it was found that Earth
Does not weigh more or less
It's pound for pound
Nothing at its best

The astrologists pitched in
To fantasize that the world of men
Would grow to twice its size
As we increased the population

When the teachers and preachers
Conferred about the origin
Of the World and its creatures
They eliminated evolution as a sin

Then emerged that English man Charles Darwin
Who tested his thesis that the World was from a seed
From which all life evolved on the scene
Much like a monkey or a weed

To this most scientists and theologians disagreed
With other theories decreed
Such as a solar event
Much like the preachers' advent

As the world turns today
There is no agreement or solution
To the origination of man and its parlay
Other than religion or science are the absolution

So the poets and speculators
Write and bet on Earth's
Motions and emotions
Tides and human prides
Caught up
As the world turns
You neither see it or feel it
But we're all turning with it
On the same trip
Held here by the same spirit
And leaving by the same crypt

Transcending into another time
Just blending words
Into a rhyme
About the sublime

Forming words for afterwards
As life adjourns
And the mind learns
To listen

To the eulogy

As the world turns
And Hell burns
And Heaven yearns
Its flock likely returns

On its trip
From the White hole to the Black hole
And back again to where it all begins
In the flight through the solar winds

FALLING STAR

You're so great
You're so bright
Part of fate
Out of sight

Passing by
You sail
Through the sky
No mortal trail

Be ye good
Or be ye bad
To which you should
You will be glad

Tip the scales
And think you're big
Puff your sails
And shine your rig

Strut around
Be the most
But pound for pound
You're a ghost

Shallower yet
Than skin is deep
Cape all wet
And critics bleep

What goes up
Must come down
Spilling from the cup
All along the ground

Destiny has been dealt
As a hand
Bloody with a welt
Warnings felt to understand

If ignored
Watch out below
The star isn't restored
It doesn't glow no more

Fallen from
Its highest place
Deaf and dumb
Lost in space

Until it crashes
Into a fate
That smashes
Hopes once so great

An ordinary
Example of the equality
Of the journey
To and fro by a falling identity

A star once rising
Falls from the sky
For criticizing
The family guy

CROOKED FOOTPRINTS

Alas footprints
Upon the grass
Taking a step or two
Upon the morning dew

Looking back
At my track
It's got the mark
Of a blind man
Walking in the dark

Why can't I see
Where I'm going
Without knowing
Why can't I get there
To take your dare

But I swear
The gentle air
Blows me away
To yesterday
And a day dream
Once a nightmare

Walking in these shoes
Hoping I don't lose
Cause my track
Can't circle back

To where it used to be
Like a ship wrecked
Upon a sea
I must turn around
Despite running aground

The futile sound of my heart
As I start
To repent
My crooked shoeprints unsure
Zig Zagging towards my next adventure

My Maker didn't make the prints
As the Judge of my decisions
There are hindsight events
Which incriminate my destinations

If I blame circumstance
I will never deal with the cracks
Like having ants in my pants
My crooked footprints display the facts

Straighten the gait
Sight your destination on goals
Believe it is better to wait
For the better path and lower tolls

And you'll be rewarded with cleaner souls

SMILE ME A RAINBOW

Rain pours down your face
Thunder is there without a trace
But wind and stormy weather
Has brought us back together

But there's still that pain
That makes us want to rain
So if you want to let me know
Just smile me a rainbow

Dry your eyes and dab your nose
Kiss me long and hold me close
See it's just the same
As we were before the rains came

It seems to be a part of being
Together one more time
Despite the storm brewing
We seem to be fine

So all I ask
Is let me know
Please lift the mask
And smile me a rainbow

Then as the sun comes out
The birds of a feather
Dance and shout
Goodbye stormy weather

Now that the seasons are together
At the end of that rainbow
Gold will rain down come hither
On the spot where true lovers go

Then they don't have to roam
It's known as the gee sin drome

COMPETITORS

The gladiators fought for their lives until they died
The Court Jesters gave the crowds their pride
The Explorers found new lands
The Pilgrims brought civilization to the bands
The Climbers conquered Mr. Everest with their hands

These men were no different than us
They were of flesh and bones
But beneath the surface
They had a purpose
That wouldn't let them go
Blood that flowed
In a different direction

They were competitors
They thrived on challenges
Whether they carried a sword
Or a back pack
It was with one thing in mind
Conquer an obstacle
Conquer the fear that goes along
With taking the risk
Flirting with Death
Like a habitual gambler

These men were few
And still are
It takes a special breed
I say
To risk everything for a scant few lines
In the History books
But maybe it was and is more
Maybe these men were chosen
Maybe the purpose they had
Was endowed to them
By the Almighty competitor

I see God in all of them
I see a spirit and a will to win
I can't believe it's happenstance
I believe certain men and women are destined
To be competitors
To be the leaders
To be the monuments
For which passages are written

I respect these men and women
I feel they've made sacrifices
To achieve what they've done
In fact to me I'tis more than that
I believe they had an emptiness
That needed to be filled
With a competitor's achievements

And in giving of them selves
We put ink in the historian's pen
To write about the most
Profound competition
Man versus himself
Woman versus herself
Men versus Women
Women versus men
Color versus color
Religion versus religion

In a country striving to free itself
Of discrimination
Bigotry
Fear of our neighbors
And distrust of our leaders
To keep us safe from being poor

In America we shall find
Despite losing some battles but not the war
We win the competition for the Greater
Good of man and woman kind

THE AUTUMN OF OUR LIVES

THE AUTUMN OF OUR LIVES

This morning
As I look out upon
The golden corn stalks
Knowing that the time
For harvest is near
I look back at the
Fading summer past

To some things held dear
The good times with the children
The feeling of warm sunshine
Carrying love to warm the heart
My poetic lines
That captured my mind

As my senses raced
To meet the future
And my feelings tried to
Describe the past
Now that the color is changing

In the trees
Readying the eyes for
Nature's sleep
It gives birth
To these memories
Memories of what the summer was

With no thoughts of what it wasn't
Blessed be the Autumn of our lives
That gives rest for a new generation
And the rebirth of another summer sun

Despite the throes of Winter
Of our seasonal lives

BAD BOSS BLUES

For years and years
I cried those wet less tears
Told what to do
Nothing new

By the boss
Made me blue
Thought it was me
It just couldn't be

That my soul needed
To be free
Then when I got the news
That I couldn't choose

I began to realize
I had the Bad Boss Blues
It didn't take long
To write my own song

Spoken and written
Much more strong
When fired not retired
Job just lost at my cost

I'd been bossed
Pushed and shoved
Thoughts never loved
As they were said

They became dead
Just to regret on my face
Waiting to get
Pushed back in place

That was the case
Until I was able to choose
A smidgen of the good news
Yes saved from the Bad Boss Blues

Now that I look back
As I'm on track
I sometimes wonder how
I could allow

Myself to bow
To the whimsical news
Of the Bad Boss Blues
Kicking me out of the slave crews

Hallelujah I'm free
I can see what I want to be
The Bad Boss made no fool of destiny
Just a better me

HEAVEN ON EARTH

Peace of mind
Gentle smile
Soft caress
Eyes beguile

Under stress
Faith is on trial
Funny how
Heaven waits

For no one
That hesitates
To find the sun
And drink life's wine

Heaven on earth
Gives birth
Nothing more
Than the seeking mind

Nothing less than
Being kind
This is peace
Avoid the Hell

It's more than
A belief in God
Or praising the man
When there's sin

Against the commandment ten
Earth is Heaven or Hell
As the mind is sick
Or well

Like it or not we are what we got

A LIBRA

A Libra
A gentle side
A driving tide
A soft snow slide
A melting pride
A Libra is a Zebra

She smiles in the rain
She is the eye of a hurricane
She is always and never vain
She is here and there for my pain
She is love that cannot wane
She's a Libra

Make a sensual sound
Make a wrinkle into a frown
Make a square go round
Make a lost be found
Make a city from a town
God made a Libra's crown
She's a Libra

The sign of the sun
The mast of the moon
The striking of midnight
And the passing of noon
The sound of silence
Her music is in tune
She's a Libra

Eyes so green
Hair so clean
Thoughts so serene
Face so tween
Body so lean
Skin so teen
Smile so purine
That's my Libra Queen
Shari's a Libra

Kim's a Libra
Leigh's a Libra
Celena's a Libra
Grandma White was a Libra
October birthdays is a Libra

EVERGREEN

Evergreen upon the ground
What makes you green and oh so round

Never changing is your face
Aging yet without a trace

Spread you are just as tall
Winter summer spring and fall

Evergreen Evergreen upon the ground
Speak what's you secret make a sound

Be you green or be you Spruce blue
Seems you always look brand new

Needles falling limbs go sprawling
What by nature is your calling

Might it be done you suppose
You maintain your beauty a Kelly Rose

To your credit and color all about
Hymns are sung and children shout

As Christmas is made by the Evergreen
Fondest coming we've ever seen

Merry Christmas has ever been
Thank God for Jesus and the Evergreen

THE DAY YOU TOLD ME GOODBYE

I looked back and I can't remember
Any such day as that day in September
The day you told me goodbye
And I was too speechless or stupid to ask why

For I thought our love would never die
So long as we gave it a chance
And gave our waning romance
One more try

But now you're saying goodbye
And I just want to know why
Is it because the spark ran dry
Or that the spice is gone from the pie

Tell me why baby you're saying goodbye
I feel I could probably whimper you out of it
Just like you can cure a dog of its distemper
But I'm not sure that would make a difference

Because When I get near you I can see a wince
And the meaning of good sense
Is to get away
To do as you say

We parted company till another day

180 days later
I took your hand in mine
As a reprieved debtor
Slipped an engagement ring on your finger as the sign

Our life together would be divine

56 years later with
4 children
12 grandchildren
1+1 great grandsons
7 grand dogs

Thank God I started
What was imparted
Being more aware
Of the love that was there

And not out there somewhere

THE EMBARRASSED RIVER

Crossing the line between uneasy and fine
Is the trickling water of time
The river winds gently through the hills
The green hills of Illinois

As the Embarrassed River
In the landmark of Troy
Raging between Range Creek and the
The oceans it will seek

The Embarrassed River widens to a narrow point
And the drainage for the land caught
It shall anoint
Once a tributary to all points sought

And so sought to ferry traffic
It's now not much more
Than a drip to pour
If it were put in a cup

And allowed to drain from a horse tank
The only reason I have taken the time to notice
Is because of its name and the chirping of the locust
Which occupy the trees along the bank

Cutting through the breeze
I've passed it so many times
Without bothering to breathe
Or think of a rhyme

About this unusual landmark
That later I gasped on a lark
That I had to park
And stand there looking it over in the dark

That prompted these words to bring
This silly little thing called the Embarrassed River
Nothing less than the bottom of my quiver
To become the theme to sing

Because I just happened to wonder why
A river would make me cry
And I suppose that arrow
Try as it may to land

May just fly forever
So the Embarrassed River
Doesn't run dry
And eventually die

Bringing rain to my tent
And dryness to our plain
So this embarrassment
Isn't in vain

PARENTS KNOW

Parents know and the teachers too
Children don't say just what you want to hear
If they listen for the children's cue
They put it their way with very little fear

They tell it like it is
And tell you what they know
About how they did on the quiz
And how things really go

Of course you got to ask them
Then listen for the truth
Not bent by whim
But more inclined by youth

To carry stories home
To tell you how they feel
For their little minds roam
When you spin their inner wheel

And it's really very simple
To find out what they think
Just watch for the dimple
Or how their eyes shall blink

This all tells you something
If you'll only take time to contemplate
How important it is that the school bell ring
And that your children don't be late

It's all in the parents' attitudes
That can shrink to mere platitudes
To the point of misunderstanding
What education alludes
And keeps our teachers banding

For if we like what we see
It's almost imperative
That we express our gratuity
For they too have to live

And when we thank them for what they really are
Or criticize them when they've gone too far
We should make it in an understanding manner
And help to build the spirit
So in learning our children never fear it

And to those teachers that will take the time
And we know who they are
They're the clapper in the chime
And the twinkle in the emerging star

For they put knowledge from the written page
In our children so when they go to college
They will know right from wrong
And how to adapt and belong

Yes we know the good ones
We can feel it sense it
From our daughters and sons
Even when they wince it

And by the way they talk
When you suggest they speak about their teacher
Or the way they hesitate and balk
Even their eyes can praise or impeach her

So Mrs. Smith let me say this
How you're helping our daughter grow
And be that more mature Miss
Of this Shari and I certainly realize and know

Thank you for being more
That's why we appreciate you so
As you've helped us open the door
To the future of Kelli Jo

COMING DOWN

I can't count the ways
That they get high these days
But what goes up
Must come down
Sticks and stones all around

Getting high
Feeling good
Don't know why
They think they should

But it's there
It's always been
Don't they care
To try again

It's not hard
To hug a habit
Smoke the yard
And kill a rabbit

But coming down
That's unbelievably hard
Pound for pound
A head to retard

A hurricane
A bit of rain
Mind insane
A lot of pain

Coming down is hard to do
Especially if it's you

But if you don't
Come down to write your will
I'm sure Heaven won't
But Hell will with a pill

Because angels are high
The natural way
Still able to sigh
As they fly past Judgement Day

So Satan is waiting alone
For those that fly
Too high until they die
In the no fly zone

Coming down to his fiery stew
So hard to do
When it's all that's left to you
Don't you wish you'd never flew

Leaving behind straight tried and true

HOPE LIGHTS MY FIRE

Hope lights my fire with its eternal flame
Using the match of desire
No single time is the same
It may be the light of the sire

It may be a successful goal
But doing it my way
Takes hope lighting my soul
To hope like faith we are not born

Because in the beginning
All a day had was a morn
And the morn alone had no way of winning
No way of winning the reborn

The desires and determinations
Without the human bent
Exercising real vibrations
The violin with no strings or accent

Takes away the mortal choice
The choice to have hope
The will to have a voice
With more than the words of the Pope

As the essence of strife
For fire and brimstones
Cooling over a hot life
Way beyond TV and telephones

Hope lights the match of my desire
Yes it's the voice of the choir
And the pulpit for the sire
Where the flame of life gets me higher

And my ego is burning to be the squire
Ambition aggression dissention
Takes the destination then retire
Takes as much faith as apprehension

Because fear lights the fire
Under the hope and desire

FOOL'S GOLD

FOOL'S GOLD

Day dreams
Night dreams
Who believes
In what it seems
No fool can feel
No more
Than what is real

Don't tell me your story
Don't read my palm
I don't believe in glory
Nor that destiny is calm
Or the happy ending of a sad story
As my dreams disappear at dawn

Who can sell fool's gold
Into a fortune anyway
For even today is hell
And even fools will pray

Slander is in a fool's cell
Doing it the Devil's negative way
It's the fool's prey
To those who say

That dreamer's
Can't make it come out
Their way

What I say it's the doubt
Of destiny
Which to many
Fail to pray
For dreams each day
Keeping nightmares for the night

Maybe they won't exist at sunset
When Goals are set
By those who will place the bet
For they can see
Day dreams do become reality

That's why we call them
Day Dreams
Nightmares
Sunup of a new day
Sunset of a bad day
Rainbow's pot of gold
Chasing Fool's Gold

Something you can hold
Dollar bills you unfold
Fool's goals
Or
Fool's gold
Knows when to hold
Them
Never knows when to fold
Them

LIVE AS A TREE

LIFE

The tree is life and we are it's fruit
Our limbs spread to give and take
Our buds beget the perennial shoot
Our roots grope to sustain life's stake
Our bark resists the inhuman brute
Our greenery conceals the trailing wake

DEATH

The tree evolves and we are dust
Our limbs fold from their rigidity
Our buds dry to a peaceful lust
Our roots hibernate life's heredity
Our bark hardens and breaks as it must
Our greenery shrouds our longevity

AFTER

The tree evolves so may we
Our cycles somehow explain life's metaphor
Our existence is by law not by mystery
Our incarnation may be the tide that mounts the shore
Our life may be the tree that outlives history
Alas our cycle must mean life after and for evermore

NOW

The tree stands proud
We are free to live or die
We grow the apple tree endowed
We cultivate the apple pie
We sit under the leaves
We hide from the raining sky
We are the seed that reprieves

Us and the tree from what life achieves
Life death and the regeneration in the archives
Emerging for the journey of our next lives
From womb to tomb mortal time flies

Immortal life defies
Science logic religion
With its contagion *
Reincarnation

*the spreading of a harmful idea or practice

MY LOVELY

Lovely so lovely
Her eyes her face
Sweet baby Chris to kiss

Like a deep blue sky
So lovely is Chris
A lovely girl too sweet to miss

With hair soft to the touch
She's the silk of a butterfly
Teenage beauty becoming to the eye

Emerging from a cocoon a miss
Made by Her mother and I
Grownup is this sweet little Chris

A monarch so lovely
She spreads her wings
To depart from me

Mature is that lovely Chris we will miss

To fly away
Into a soft misty rain
Before our eyes
Which reflect our pain

Flying to her mate
A full life to live
As a lovely miss
I used to kiss

No longer just my baby Chris
That nature's twist
Is now a womanist
I guess I won't have to miss

With her sweet babies to kiss

CARTWHEELS

Running spinning with no beginning
Bending spending knows no ending
Slipping tripping made for whipping
That's the cart-wheeler's arcade

Faking taking could be they're afraid
Creatures preachers alike they call
Be they mighty or be they small
For the harder they flip the harder they fall

Turning churning that's their yearning
Never learning in spite of spurning
Sighing crying almost flying
There is so much useless about their trying
That's the cart-wheeler's promenade

So when you find someone turning endless big deals
Remember how good it feels
To turn out more than useless cart wheels
Or slipping and sliding on banana peels

All it takes is a skilled gymnast
Doing backflips and multiple front flips
To put the imposter in the past
Doing meaningful program tips

Skill comes in many forms
As does an Olympian the theologian
Knowing why no ordinary scorns
Are responsible for being a surgeon

Doing impressive cart-wheels
More likely than not there is
As past failure reveals
A skill called the Wiz

Hiding as a skill that life conceals
Under the meshing of a mind's wheels

THAT'S ROMANCE

What is romance
Is it a personality trait or vice
That a person is willing to sacrifice
Their own welfare as the price

To serve another
For the likes of their mother
Or the love of their brother
With feelings that don't smother

There stands that lonely man
Upon the corner of the crowd
He seems to be content not to understand
But as you look closer the eyes aren't proud

If you ask him if he's happy
What will he say
Chances are he would say "I'm a man of no love"
"I'm a man that forgot making time for romance
I mishandled my chance with a push and shove"

"There are reasons I have no romance no wife"
"I'm of a mind bent by time"
"Carrying this burden to the end"
"With no romance that's my senseless crime"

"My retort to you is this my friend"
"Why can't you change before it's too late"
"You've got the mind and heart to bend"
"Just change your personal trait"

God help that lonely man he's blue
He has forsaken his chance
To share his life for romance
Among the many who are jealous of the few

Not a personality trait
But a person who has to sacrifice
Their own welfare at any price
To advance chance over circumstance or happenstance

That's romance

ON THE WINGS OF THE DOVE

The story has it
The seed of peace
Was planted
By a beautiful white dove
Unscathed by
Warlord times

Peace was planted in the sand
In most every land
Flown in on the flapping wings of freedom
As it grew it faced
The rigors and resistance of mankind

Growing in spite of unfertile minds
As a turbulent history unwinds
Along the way there were
Droughts and floods
To erode the once deep seeded roots
Exposing peace to the inhumane holocaust

The pressures of revolution and evolution
Put the survival of peace in jeopardy
The dove on winged prayers
Returned to watch over its sentinel
Imprisoned by a sinful world
Cremating the future and consuming its own

But each time
The pressures became relentless
As man hated man
Inconspicuously each feather
Pulled from the wings of peace
Destroyed the roots the very roots
Of what had been planted there

The times they were turbulent
And they have been relentless
The dove's return flight became
More and more infrequent
Bare wings began to slap
Against the sides of inhumanity

The dove became scarred by senseless wars
The history was written that no
Day of Judgement would
Befall mortals as long as the Dove
Returned

Now that we've waited breathless
For its return after all these years
We hear a flurry of
A flurry of frantic movement
We see out of the corner of reality
A grayish figure flailing at a
Extreme headwind
Of ideological opposition

As this figure struggles into sight
Clearer to the eye
We detect no feathers on the frame
My God it looks so lame
Will it survive or die of rejection
The War Hawks have always been against her
Waiting to have the thrill
It's their turn to make the kill

With a fury unparalleled in our times
The hawks attack
The dove dives towards the Earth
Towards the end of peace so profound
But behold it lights without a sound
And lays an egg upon the ravaged ground
Hatched in His image
Behold the Dove has risen

It lives again
It shall fly for peace once more
This wingless Dove saves
The soul that braves
So those War Hawks shall decease

And wars will cease
For peace to
Rule
Celebrated by the Christmas Yule

PLAY ME

I am a song upon the heart strings
Without words

I am a dream under the pillow
Oh so real

I am the tune
Yet to be heard

You're the instrument
Only you can set me free so

Sing along with our
Family choir

As you would
Father and Motherhood

I am your feelings
Not yet achieved

I am the thoughts before the lines
Not yet conceived

I am an instrument
In your hands to unwind

I am an idea in your mind
Yet to be believed

Play me

To make love music
Forever is what we seek

I am life to your roots
I am the leaves to your family tree

Play for me

You are my wife
My most valuable companionship

Play house with me

WHAT WOULD IT BE

What would the nighttime be
Without the light of thee
What would the bedside be
Without the bed with me

And what would the heart of you be
If it weren't for my love for thee
Would it be living without fright
Or would it be doing it right

What would a fall to injustice
Mean to me
When the future would
Be a futile memory

No nothing could be
Nor would you be here with me
If not for the evolution of nature
Dictating our future

No love couldn't be
It wouldn't be
Without the three
Jesus you and me

So how do you take this opportunity
And turn it into a happy healthy prosperous life
Call it luck of the draw
Being in the right place at the right time

Or it is my responsibility to answer
What would it be
Without me
And that is the answer of our mystery

What would the blossom be
Without the rose and magnolia tree
What would Jesus be
Without mankind to free

My answer is
There would be no Jerry Lee
This very special me
Without my children love and Shari
The wonder of the trinity

PAINT ME A RAINBOW

Daddy... Daddy dear
What's a rainbow
What's a reindeer
Daughter Daughter dear

Listen well listen clear
I will show you
Never fear
Looky... looky here

I will show
The rainbow is no reindeer
Daddy... Daddy dear
I'm confused
It's not clear

Daughter please wipe
Away your tear
I will show you
Come in near

See this ribbon
In your hair
Take it out
Hold it there

Splash it with
Your paint so true
Dash it with
Pink yellow and blue

Add some lavender
To the hue
Like the rain through
The sunny dew

Take it carefully
In your hand
Hold it up
Make it stand

Twist it tight
Let it fan
Shake it loose
When you can

Making purple
Out of blue
Then when it's dry
Colors pretty to the eye

Tie it to a mast way up high
In the sky
Where Santa's reindeers
Can learn to fly

And then with your red
Put some ears on their head
And as the wind blows
Paint the reddest on the leader's nose

Flying above the rainbow
We call him the red nosed reindeer
With gifts for all who know
They've been good all this year

Now daughter... daughter dear
Do you understand
Have I made it clear
How to paint a rainbow's fan

Yes daddy… daddy dear
It's different from the reindeer's nose
Since the reindeer is for that time of year
And the rainbow is for this prose

With the fairytale of the red nose forever deer

GRADUATION OF SMOKE

I took my first smoke
What a joke
Mimicked and copied
Them ole folk

Yes I understand
That this weed habit
Is the making of your band
And you're going to grab it

It takes a crazy bloke
To take up and have a smoke
But when you're feeling bad
And almost broke

There's the urge to stoke
Burn some meth
And snort the coke
Till you're broke

Then taking your last breath
So close to death
Till you've awoke
To how senseless it is to smoke

Break the habit
Throw down that smoke
Look around at the other folk
Wised up as their lungs invoke

To the will to smoke
Take your tobacco poke
Let it soak
Until good senses provoke

That your lungs need
Before you've gone up in smoke
A gasp of fresh air not some weed
With no will to evoke

Contrary to conventional knowledge
The entry point of drug addiction
Is jumping off that smoker ledge
Into that polluted air of inhalation

High school or being a fool it leads to devastation
By graduating from smoking to an addict's sensation

BROKEN WINDMILLS

BROKEN WINDMILLS

Broken windmills are standing in the farm yard
Marking the progress we've made away from nature
Once they pumped the water and churned the lard
While the farmers pushed their plows to plant
With no thought of the future

Crops were cared for by loving hands
The backbone of the country and feeding a nation
Making America stronger than most other lands
Having more to enjoy without ration

The horses were our shoulders
Pulling us along behind
Representing our mobility while carrying soldiers
And weapons to get those treaties signed

The common folk were the very spoke
Of our country's stability
They handled the scythe and donned the yoke
Forming and farming our simple society

The family planted the seed to bloom
Raising the children with oh so much pride
Setting them upon the world none too soon
Having known simple pleasures family tied

The hand feed shuttle kept us warm
Weaving patterns into our memories
Accustomed to each winter storm
And never ignoring our love of humility

Now the windmill stands broken in the yard
With no need for its practicality
The horses once so proud now stand scarred
As they've been replaced by auto mobility

The crops still feed the hordes
But now its machines that take the burden
Replacing the common folk with greedy land lords
Changing the attitude to "pay me no uncertain"

The shuttle still is doing twice its duty
Putting its wares upon the family members scattered
But now it's more mechanical with less beauty
Forgotten is the feeling of being together
And how it once mattered
This represents progress and try as we must
We seem to be losing to our insecurity
Forgetting the principles in which we trust
The principles of work love and family

And the pursuit of healthful happiness
Faith in God safety on Earth
While keeping our wealth from our success
So we have and save human net worth

Don't you think it might help
To mend the broken windmills
And our country's mental state
By remembering these principles
And such symbols that made America great

Built on a constitution and the broken windmills fate

180 YESTERDAYS

Passing me by
Like I'm standing still
Passing thoughts
Are for time to kill

Yesterday's gone
With each succeeding dawn
And it's true
That's why I'm blue

It seems like 180 yesterdays
Since you said goodbye
Tomorrow's only filled
With sorrow… I want to die

If I can't trade today
For yesterday
180 suns away
Turn me around

Turn me back
Let me go
Let me know
180 days a year ago

To and fro
Don't you know
Feeling high
Then feeling low

Can't get back
A year ago
Hang it up
Throw it down

Let it go
Without a sound
There's no way
To be found

To get back yesterday

To wit I just heard
An encouraging word
You want to reverse that fact
And take me back
If that's true
Let me be very clear
What your departure did do
Was to make me reappear

As 180 times more appreciative of you

FATHER NOAH

FATHER NOAH

Father Noah saying prayers
Why do you bother
No one really cares
Listen listen don't
You see
It's the mission
To relieve the sea of Galilee

Spoken that's your word
Is it a token of the afterward
Harken to the call
Could be you're barken' up the wrong wall
Father Noah is it true
Would it be better to be Christian Catholic or Jew
Sinner… sinner just let it be
Repent to be the winner
Tis of thee

Noah that's my name
Father time don't you know
Redemption is my game
Just believe faithfully
Father Noah let me know
Bring me hither is it so
Dreamer… dreamer there is hope
Follow the redeemer to the Pope
Father Noah will it be that
Your mission is propagate to procreate

Father Noah if you please
Take me further upon your breeze
Children… children climb aboard
Cleanse your sin and drop the sword
Father Noah launch your Ark
God acts with foul weather
So we must embark

With all the procreating animals on the Ark

2 cattle in their stalls
2 horses in their harness
2 lions and lioness
2 elephants in their places
2 giraffes nuzzling faces
2 tigers calm and restrained
2 birds in their nests refrained
2 insects in the fertile plants
2 sloths eating the 10 ants
2 reptiles in their habitat
2 lambs and goats herded intact
2 of all other species
Dwelling on the Ark despite the feces
Every one of the best

Captain deploy the sails and rudders for each wave's crest

Mortals… mortals hold on fast
Close the portal your fate is cast
The boatswain has the mast
Captain Peter bound the main
Bring it aft cleft the swain
Angel… Angel the Lord awaits
The Ark shall scale the Pearly Gates
Souls please do employ
We're almost there
Land ahoy
As Angel carols fill the air

Moses took the dare
And moved his mountain
Before we could spare
The time to take on Satan
With the sermon on the mount
We killed sin all about

Father Noah thanks to thee
We're in Holy Heaven
Next to Jesus on your knee
With all of earth's goods for day seven
To sustain life once again
As the flood waters descend
The new world begins

Void of sins
For sake of those left behind
Our Earth has combined
The chosen few who will redesign

The mortal weakness thus resigned

ECLIPSE

The sun is the only sign of perfection
In our world
It appears every dawn
Perfectly on schedule

It traverses the sky
Each day
Never deterred until it sets
Upon the imperfection of our lives

As I think about it
I can think of nothing else
That's as stable
And more profoundly affixed

It seems that it's the only symbol
Of security
It doesn't visually disintegrate
With time or before our eyes

It's never off schedule
It's always there when we need it
Representing the very nature of life
The hope of the future

We know it burns perpetually
Rekindled by the spirit of tomorrow
That we call God
The eternal flame burns right in our minds

Of all those that face it
Hoping it won't cease
But there upon
Every 60 years

Earth passing
That barren asteroid
Called the moon
When Day becomes night too soon

Eclipsing our life line
Across our sun
With the only imperfection
Until the light of night is done

The sun has won

THE END IS THE BEGINNING

Towards the end of Judgment day
What does God say
For he only speaks
To he who seeks

He pronounces with a natural reason
That beauty is in the closing decision
For tomorrow how fortunate we are
To live among angels… amidst our own star

Closing into darkness the spirit finds its way
As Goodness speaks to the heart's decay
Cutting through space to another time
A continuum is what we will find

Marked in the sky as searching afar
Quiet but alive is the soul of our rising star
Believe it will happen once more
Behind the curtain of now

Gone forever are moments of wow
And questions of how
Only to covet the path of the metaphor
The cycle is what it treks as bodies decay

Moving into another continuum's door
Seeking the horizons of peace in the milky-way
Alas the end is the beginning
In the Heaven of ever…. more

Heaven on earth is what is in store
For the winner and reformed sinner
Spinning our own DNA web
As the sign of that mental state

Linking us to the spiritual ebb
Of our immortal fate
For all of mankind
To find the undiscovered planet
Called the mind

Connecting us all to the other nine
A mental Solar system divine
Truly the Tenth Wonder of our mortal confine

Invitation
Now that you have ventured
This far off your planet into the world of my mind
Are we more nurtured
And attached by the wonder of rhyme

If so
email me
jerry.l.rhoads@gmail.com
for the sequels

Edwards Brothers Malloy
Thorofare, NJ USA
October 13, 2016